I0448378

May 2013

EXPORT-IMPORT BANK

Additional Analysis and Information Could Better Inform Congress on Exposure, Risk, and Resources

May 2013

GAO Highlights

Highlights of GAO-13-620, a report to congressional committees

EXPORT-IMPORT BANK

Additional Analysis and Information Could Better Inform Congress on Exposure, Risk, and Resources

Why GAO Did This Study

Ex-Im helps U.S. firms export goods and services by providing a range of financial products. Following the 2007-2009 financial crisis, increased demand resulted in rapid increases in Ex-Im's portfolio and exposure. The Export-Import Bank Reauthorization Act of 2012 reauthorized Ex-Im through fiscal year 2014 and, as a condition of raising Ex-Im's exposure limit in 2013, required Ex-Im to prepare a report with a business plan and analyses of key operational elements. The act also directed GAO to analyze the Business Plan. This report discusses the extent to which Ex-Im's Business Plan and analyses (1) justify bank exposure limits; (2) evaluate the risk of loss associated with the increased exposure limit, changing composition of exposure, and compliance with congressional mandates; and (3) analyze the adequacy of Ex-Im resources to manage authorizations and comply with congressional mandates. GAO reviewed Ex-Im's Business Plan, analyses, and other reports, and interviewed Ex-Im officials.

What GAO Recommends

Ex-Im should (1) adjust its forecasting model based on previous experience, (2) assess and report the sensitivity of the exposure forecast model to key assumptions and estimates, (3) routinely report the financial performance of subportfolios supporting congressional mandates, and (4) provide Congress with additional information on the resources associated with meeting mandated targets. Ex-Im concurred with our recommendations.

View GAO-13-620. For more information, contact Lawrance L. Evans, Jr. at (202) 512-4802 or EvansL@gao.gov.

What GAO Found

While the Export-Import Bank (Ex-Im) Business Plan reported that Ex-Im's exposure limits were appropriate, the forecasting process used to reach this conclusion has weaknesses. Congress increased the Ex-Im exposure limit—the limit on Ex-Im's total aggregate outstanding amount of financing—to $120 billion in 2012, with provisions for additional increases to $130 billion in 2013 and $140 billion in 2014. Although Ex-Im's forecast model is sensitive to key assumptions, GAO found that Ex-Im did not reassess these assumptions to reflect changing conditions or conduct sensitivity analyses to assess and report the range of potential outcomes. GAO used historical data in lieu of these assumptions and found that Ex-Im's forecast of exposure could be higher than the limit set by Congress for 2014. GAO's cost guidance calls for agencies' assumptions and forecasts to be supported by historical data and experience, and a sensitivity analysis, which can assess the effect of changes in assumptions. Because Ex-Im has not taken these steps, the reliability of its forecasts is diminished. This is of particular concern because Ex-Im projects that its outstanding financing in the future will be closer to its exposure limit than it has been historically. Consequently, any forecast errors could result in the bank having to take actions, such as delaying financing for creditworthy projects, to avoid exceeding its limit.

The Business Plan provided limited analysis of Ex-Im's risk of loss. First, Ex-Im did not provide some forecast data because of pending Office of Management and Budget (OMB) approval of key analyses. For example, Ex-Im did not include conclusions on Ex-Im's overall risk of loss and risk by industry. Second, Ex-Im included only limited analysis to support its conclusions that changes in its portfolio—including subportfolios of transactions supporting congressional mandates for small business, sub-Saharan Africa, and renewable energy—would not affect its risk of loss. In addition, Ex-Im has not routinely analyzed or reported the risk rating and default rate of subportfolios that respond to these mandates, although their performance may differ from the overall portfolio. OMB and banking regulator guidance call for entities, including federal agencies, to be able to provide comprehensive information by subportfolio, product, and other financial performance metrics. By not routinely analyzing and reporting financial performance for mandated transactions, Ex-Im decreases its ability to evaluate such performance at the subportfolio level and inform Congress of related risks.

The Business Plan provided limited analysis of the adequacy of Ex-Im's resources and ability to meet congressional mandates. From 2008 through 2012, Ex-Im's administrative resources remained relatively flat as its portfolio grew. Ex-Im does not expect to meet its small business or renewable energy mandate targets in 2013 or 2014. These mandate targets are fixed to a percentage of the dollar value of Ex-Im's total authorizations. Although Ex-Im has dedicated resources to support these mandates, as Ex-Im authorizations have grown, the growth in mandate targets has outpaced Ex-Im's increasing support. Ex-Im projects that the targets will continue to outpace its growth in support through 2014. Mandate transactions also are resource-intensive and Ex-Im's ability to expand its renewable energy portfolio may be constrained by the size of the overall market. Communicating the effect of percentage-based targets on Ex-Im's resources and ability to achieve its goals to external stakeholders, such as Congress, is consistent with federal internal control standards.

_____ United States Government Accountability Office

Contents

Abbreviations

Ex-Im	U.S. Export-Import Bank
FTE	full-time equivalent
IT	information technology
OMB	Office of Management and Budget

GAO U.S. GOVERNMENT ACCOUNTABILITY OFFICE

441 G St. N.W.
Washington, DC 20548

May 30, 2013

The Honorable Tim Johnson
Chairman
The Honorable Mike Crapo
Ranking Member
Committee on Banking, Housing, and Urban Affairs
United States Senate

The Honorable Jeb Hensarling
Chairman
The Honorable Maxine Waters
Ranking Member
Committee on Financial Services
House of Representatives

The Export-Import Bank (Ex-Im) serves as the official export credit agency of the United States, providing a range of financial products for U.S. exporters and their customers to support the export of U.S. goods and services, thereby supporting U.S. jobs. Following the financial crisis of 2007-2009, increased demand for Ex-Im authorizations (caused by a retreat of private-sector lenders from the market) led to rapid increases in the size of Ex-Im's portfolio and changes in its portfolio composition.[1] While Ex-Im has been "self-sustaining" for appropriations purposes since fiscal year 2008—financing its operations from receipts collected from its customers—it must operate within the parameters and limits authorized by Congress, including congressional mandates that it support small business and promote sub-Saharan African and environmentally beneficial exports.[2]

The Export-Import Bank Reauthorization Act of 2012 (the Reauthorization Act) reauthorized the bank through 2014 and increased the limit on its total aggregate outstanding loans, guarantees, and insurance—the Ex-Im exposure limit—to $120 billion in 2012, and to $130 billion in 2013 and

---

[1]An authorization is an export financing transaction for which Ex-Im has granted credit approval.

[2]All years in this report are federal fiscal years unless otherwise indicated.

GAO-13-620 Export-Import Bank

$140 billion in 2014, if certain conditions are met.[3] As one condition to increasing the exposure limit for 2013, the reauthorization required that Ex-Im submit a report by September 30, 2012, that included a business plan and analyses:

- estimating and justifying the appropriate exposure limit;
- estimating future growth by industry sector, product type, and key market;[4]
- analyzing the risk of loss from the estimated exposure limit by industry sector, product type, and key market;
- analyzing its ability to meet congressional mandates under the proposed exposure limit and the risk of loss associated with meeting those mandates;[5] and
- analyzing the adequacy of its resources under the proposed exposure limit, including resources for required economic impact analyses.

In response to the congressional requirement, Ex-Im completed and submitted a report that, according to Ex-Im officials, generally relied on data from existing Ex-Im analyses. The reauthorization further directed GAO to analyze Ex-Im's report.[6]

This report discusses the extent to which Ex-Im's Business Plan and analyses (1) justify bank exposure limits; (2) evaluate Ex-Im's risk of loss associated with the increased exposure limit, the changing composition of exposure, and compliance with congressional mandates; and (3) analyze

---

[3]Pub. L. No. 112-122, § 3, 126 Stat. 350, 351 (2012). Ex-Im's exposure limit will be increased to $130 billion in 2013 and $140 billion in 2014 if certain statutory criteria are met.

[4]Ex-Im identified nine key markets on which to focus: Brazil, Colombia, India, Indonesia, Mexico, Nigeria, South Africa, Turkey, and Vietnam. These countries were selected based on factors including the size of the export market for U.S. companies, projected economic growth, anticipated infrastructure demand, and need for Ex-Im financing.

[5] The law specified that the Business Plan address Ex-Im's small business, sub-Saharan Africa, and carbon policy mandates. See Pub. L. No. 112-122, § 4. The carbon policy was not a congressional mandate; however, Ex-Im interpreted the carbon policy mandate in its Business Plan to refer to a congressional requirement that Ex-Im notify Congress of projects that will generate more greenhouse gases than bank-supported projects generated on average during the preceding 3 years. See Pub. L. No. 112-74, 125 Stat. 1191 for the greenhouse gas notification requirement.

[6]The act requires us to review and report on the Business Plan by June 1, 2013. Pub. L. No. 112-122 § 4(b).

the adequacy of Ex-Im resources to manage authorizations and comply with congressional mandates under the proposed exposure limits.

To assess the extent to which Ex-Im's Business Plan and analyses justify exposure limits, we reviewed Ex-Im's Business Plan and methodology, the model Ex-Im used to forecast exposure, source data on authorizations, and met with Ex-Im officials. To assess the exposure model, we compared its projections of exposure and authorizations with actual results. To assess Ex-Im's forecast of repayments, we compared Ex-Im's assumptions with previous data on the share of short-term transactions in the Ex-Im portfolio and calculated Ex-Im's exposure using alternative assumptions about short-term percentage and repayment terms. We assessed the procedures and assumptions Ex-Im used in its Business Plan forecast of exposure against GAO standards for developing estimates.[7]

To assess the extent to which Ex-Im's Business Plan and analyses evaluate the risk of loss associated with Ex-Im's increased exposure limit, the changing composition of exposure, and compliance with congressional mandates, we reviewed Ex-Im's data and documentation—including financial performance data, annual reports, and quarterly default rate reports—and previous GAO and Ex-Im Inspector General reports. To further examine Ex-Im's risk of loss evaluation in the plan, we examined weighted-average risk ratings and default rate data for fiscal years 2008 and 2012 that Ex-Im compiled for us at the subportfolio level, including by industry, product, key market, and congressional mandates. To assess the reliability of these data, we reviewed and checked them against previous Ex-Im reporting and consulted the data reviews conducted for another recent GAO report.[8] We found the data to be sufficiently reliable for the purpose of providing context for the financial performance of the overall portfolio and subportfolios in each year. To evaluate Ex-Im's risk management, we compared its risk management and analysis practices against federal banking regulator guidance on financial performance

---

[7]GAO, *GAO Cost Estimating and Assessment Guide: Best Practices for Developing and Managing Capital Program Costs*, GAO-09-3SP (Washington, D.C.: March 2009).

[8]GAO, *Export-Import Bank: Recent Growth Underscores Need for Continued Improvements in Risk Management*, GAO-13-303 (Washington, D.C.: Mar. 28, 2013).

reporting, Office of Management and Budget (OMB) guidance on federal credit programs, and GAO's standards for internal control.[9]

To assess the extent to which Ex-Im's Business Plan and analyses analyze the adequacy of Ex-Im resources to manage authorizations and comply with congressional mandates under the proposed exposure limits, we reviewed previous GAO and Ex-Im Inspector General reports. We also reviewed relevant Ex-Im documents, including Congressional Budget Justifications, annual reports, the Ex-Im charter, and other plans, performance reports, policies, and procedures. We found the data in these reports to be sufficiently reliable for the purposes of describing the growth of Ex-Im's business, size of its workforce, and amount of administrative funds requested and appropriated. To assess the reliability of these data, we reviewed and checked them against previous Ex-Im reporting and consulted the data reviews conducted for another recent GAO report.[10] We also reviewed relevant GAO and Ex-Im Inspector General reports and met with officials from Ex-Im and Ex-Im's Office of Inspector General. We compared Ex-Im's planning documents against criteria established by GAO, the Office of Personnel Management, and OMB.

We conducted this performance audit from November 2012 to May 2013 in accordance with generally accepted government auditing standards. Those standards require that we plan and perform the audit to obtain sufficient, appropriate evidence to provide a reasonable basis for our findings and conclusions based on our audit objectives. We believe that the evidence obtained provides a reasonable basis for our findings and conclusions based on our audit objectives.

---

[9] See, Board of Governors of the Federal Reserve, *Commercial Bank Examination Manual* (Washington, D.C.: March 1994). The manual is updated twice a year. See, Office of the Comptroller of the Currency, Federal Deposit Insurance Corporation, Board of Governors of the Federal Reserve, and Office of Thrift Supervision, *Interagency Guidance on Asset Securitization Activities* (Washington, D.C.: December 1999). See, Office of the Comptroller of the Currency, *Asset Securitization: Comptroller's Handbook* (Washington, D.C.: November 1997). While Ex-Im is not bound by any of the guidance cited above, it faces challenges similar to regulated private financial institutions in managing risks. See, Office of Management and Budget, Circular No. A-129 Revised, *Policies for Federal Credit Programs and Non-Tax Receivables* (2000). See GAO, *Standards for Internal Control in the Federal Government*, GAO/AIMD-00-21.3.1 (Washington, D.C.: Nov. 1, 1999); and *Internal Control Management and Evaluation Tool*, GAO-01-1008G (Washington, D.C.: Aug. 1, 2001).

[10] GAO-13-303.

Background

Ex-Im is an independent agency operating under the Export-Import Bank Act of 1945, as amended. Its mission is to support the export of U.S. goods and services, thereby supporting U.S. jobs. Ex-Im's charter states that it should not compete with the private sector. Rather, Ex-Im's role is to assume the credit and country risks that the private sector is unable or unwilling to accept, while still maintaining a reasonable assurance of repayment. As a result, when private-sector lenders reduced the availability of their financing after the 2007-2009 financial crisis, demand for Ex-Im products correspondingly increased.

Ex-Im's Functional Areas and Products

Ex-Im operates in several functional areas under the leadership of a chairman and president. Functional areas include the Small Business Group, Office of the Chief Financial Officer, Office of Resource Management, and Export Finance Group. The Export Finance Group is, in turn, subdivided into business units for certain types of transactions, such as Trade Finance, Transportation, Structured and Project Finance, and Renewable Energy.

Ex-Im offers a number of export financing products, including direct loans, loan guarantees, and export credit insurance. Ex-Im makes fixed-rate loans directly to international buyers of goods and services. These loans can be

- short-term (up to 1 year),
- medium-term (more than 1 year up to 7 years and less than $10 million), or
- long-term (including transactions of more than 7 years or $10 million and higher and longer than 1 year).

Ex-Im also guarantees loans made by private lenders to international buyers of goods or services, committing to pay the lenders if the buyers default. Like direct loans, loan guarantees may be short-, medium-, or long-term. Additionally, Ex-Im provides export credit insurance products that protect the exporter from the risk of nonpayment by foreign buyers for commercial and political reasons. This allows U.S. exporters the ability to offer foreign purchasers the opportunity to make purchases on credit. Credit insurance policies can cover a single buyer or multiple buyers and be short- or medium-term. Ex-Im's short-term insurance covers a wide range of goods, raw materials, spare parts, components, and most services on terms, in most cases, of up to 180 days. Medium-term insurance policies protect longer-term financing to international buyers of capital equipment or services, covering one or a series of shipments.

Ex-Im's long-term products are often used to finance transportation projects, in project finance transactions, and for what Ex-Im calls "structured finance." In dollar terms, transportation projects primarily support the purchase of aircraft. In project finance, Ex-Im lends to newly created project companies in foreign countries and looks to the project's future cash flows as the source of repayment. Project finance transactions have repayment terms up to 14 years, and renewable energy transactions have repayment terms up to 18 years. In structured finance transactions, Ex-Im provides direct loans or loan guarantees to existing companies located overseas. Structured finance transactions generally have repayment terms of 10 years, but some transactions may have terms of 12 years.

Ex-Im's Exposure and Portfolio Since 2008

Congress has limited the extent of potential losses to the government from Ex-Im transactions by placing a cap on Ex-Im's total amount of outstanding loans, guarantees, and insurance—the exposure limit. In the May 30, 2012 reauthorization, Congress increased Ex-Im's exposure limit to $120 billion, with provisions for additional increases to $130 billion in 2013, and $140 billion in 2014.[11] When Ex-Im authorizes additional loans, guarantees, and insurance, its exposure grows. When authorizations are repaid or cancelled, Ex-Im's exposure is reduced (see fig. 1). To forecast its exposure for the September 2012 Business Plan, Ex-Im's Office of the Chief Financial Officer used a model that took the bank's July 2012 actual exposure, added the amount of authorizations forecast by Ex-Im's business units, and subtracted the estimated amount of repayments and cancellations based on the forecast authorizations and assumptions about the portfolio composition. Ex-Im's actual exposure at the end of 2012 was $106.6 billion, and Ex-Im's Business Plan forecasts exposure to increase to $120.2 billion at the end of 2013 and $134.9 billion at the end of 2014.

---

[11] Pub. L. No. 112-122, § 3.

Figure 1: Relationship of Ex-Im Authorizations, Repayments and Cancellations, and Exposure, Fiscal Years 2012 (Actual)-2014 (Projected)

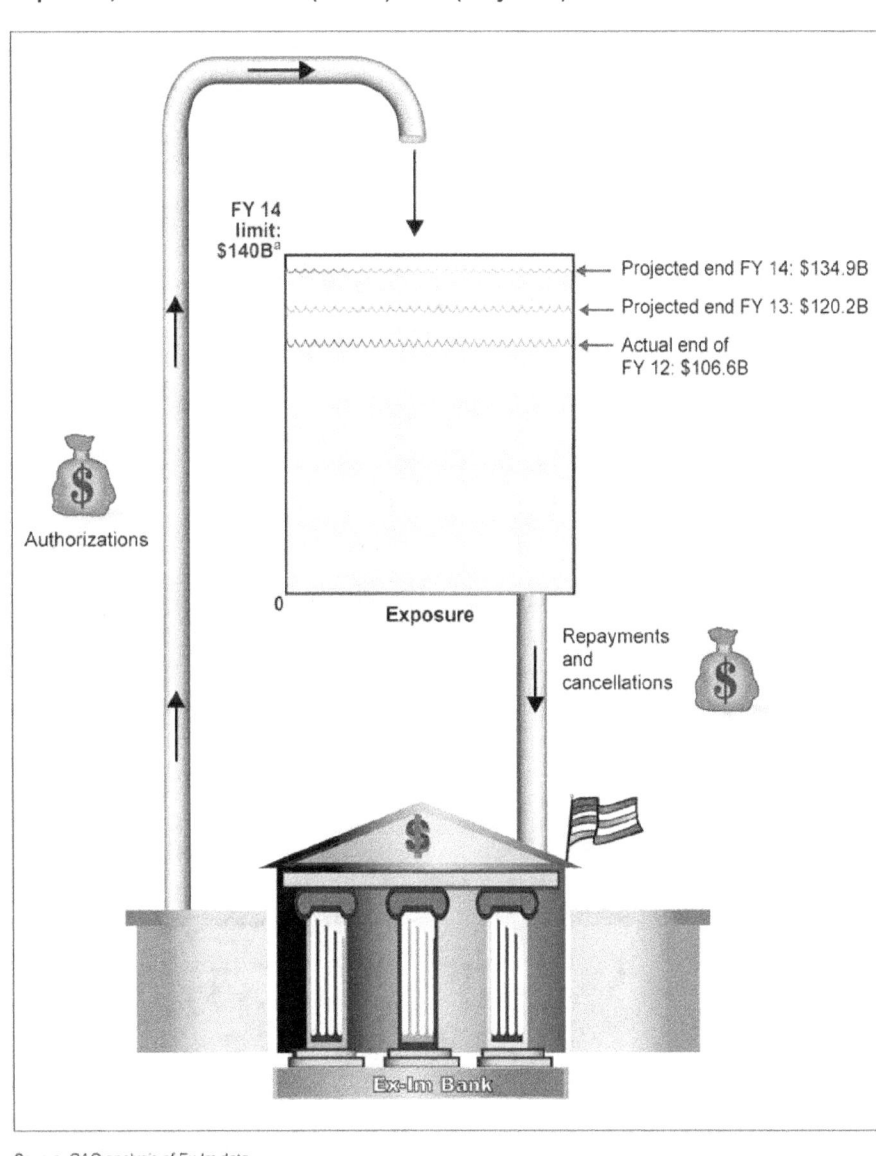

Source: GAO analysis of Ex-Im data

[a]The exposure limit was $120 billion at the end of fiscal year 2012 and $130 billion in fiscal year 2013.

Ex-Im's annual authorizations have increased. Overall, in nominal dollars, annual Ex-Im authorizations rose from $14.4 billion in 2008 to $35.8 billion in 2012 (see fig. 2). Annual authorizations for new project and structured finance transactions increased from $1.9 billion in 2008 to $12.6 billion in 2012—accounting for almost half of Ex-Im's 2012 long-term authorizations. Aircraft-related authorizations grew from $5.7 billion in 2008 to $11.9 billion in 2012—an increase of about 110 percent—and accounted for about one-third of Ex-Im's authorizations in 2012. While long-term authorizations make up the largest part of Ex-Im's portfolio in dollar terms, more than 80 percent of Ex-Im transactions are short-term.[12]

Figure 2: Ex-Im Annual Authorizations by Product Type, Fiscal Years 2008-2012

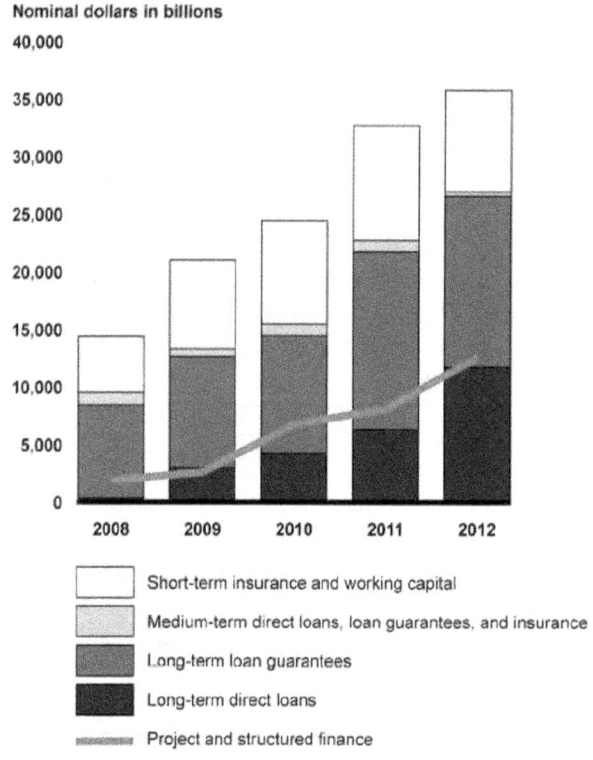

Nominal dollars in billions

Short-term insurance and working capital

Medium-term direct loans, loan guarantees, and insurance

Long-term loan guarantees

Long-term direct loans

Project and structured finance

Source: GAO analysis of Ex-Im data.

[12]As of the end of 2012, the dollar amount of medium-term insurance transactions represented less than 1 percent of the dollar amount of Ex-Im's active authorizations.

GAO-13-620 Export-Import Bank

Congressional Mandates for Ex-Im Support of Specific Businesses or Areas	While Ex-Im's business is generally driven by demand for its services from exporters, Congress has also mandated that Ex-Im support specific objectives. The Reauthorization Act requires Ex-Im to analyze its ability to meet, and its risk of loss from complying with, three congressional mandates.[13] Since the 1980s, Congress has required that Ex-Im make available a certain percentage of its total export financing each year for small business. In 2002, Congress increased the small business financing requirement from 10 to 20 percent. Congress further mandates that Ex-Im promote the expansion of its financial commitments in sub-Saharan Africa under Ex-Im's loan, guarantee, and insurance programs. Finally, in its 2012 appropriations, Congress directed that "not less than 10 percent of the aggregate loan, guarantee, and insurance authority available to [Ex-Im]... should be used for renewable energy technologies or end-use energy efficiency technologies," to which we refer as the renewable energy mandate.
Ex-Im's Risks and Risk Management	Ex-Im faces multiple risks when it extends export credit financing, including credit, political, market, concentration, foreign-currency, and operational risks. Ex-Im uses its resources to manage risks through (1) underwriting, (2) monitoring and restructuring, and (3) recovery of claims.

Underwriting: During underwriting, Ex-Im first uses its Country Limitation Schedule to determine whether it can provide financing for transactions in the country.[14] If the transaction meets the requirements of the Country Limitation Schedule, Ex-Im reviews the transaction and assigns it a risk rating based on its assessment of the creditworthiness of the obligors and to establish whether there is a reasonable assurance of repayment.[15] Ex-Im's risk ratings range from 1 (least risky) to 11 (most risky). Ex-Im generally does not authorize transactions with risk ratings over 8.

Monitoring and Restructuring: Ex-Im updates the risk ratings of medium- and long-term transactions above $1 million at least annually to reflect any changes in credit risk. Ex-Im also may restructure individual

---

[13]Pub. L. No. 112-122, § 4(a)(3).

[14]The Country Limitation Schedule specifies the types of transactions eligible for financing in each country and the conditions under which they are eligible.

[15]We use the term "obligor" to refer to entities that are contractually obligated to make payments to satisfy the terms of an Ex-Im export credit product.

Definitions of risks faced by Ex-Im:

- **Credit risk.** The risk that an obligor may not have sufficient funds to service its debt or be willing to service its debt even if sufficient funds are available.
- **Political risk.** The risk of nonrepayment resulting from expropriation of the obligor's property, war, or inconvertibility of the obligor's currency into U.S. dollars.
- **Market risk.** The risk of loss from declining prices or volatility of prices in the financial markets. Market risk can arise from shifts in macroeconomic conditions, such as productivity and employment, and from changes in expectations about future macroeconomic conditions.
- **Concentration risk.** Risk stemming from the composition of a credit portfolio. Concentration risk comes into being through an uneven distribution of credits within a portfolio. Ex-Im faces three types of concentration risk:
  - **Industry concentration.** The risk that events could negatively affect not only one obligor but also many obligors in the same industry simultaneously.
  - **Geographic concentration.** The risk that events could negatively affect not only one obligor but many obligors simultaneously across a country or region.
  - **Obligor concentration.** The risk that defaults from a small number of obligors will have a major adverse impact on the portfolio because they account for a large share of the portfolio.
- **Foreign-currency risk.** The risk of loss as a result of appreciation or depreciation in the value of a foreign currency in relation to the U.S. dollar in Ex-Im transactions denominated in that foreign currency.
- **Operational risk.** The risk of loss resulting from inadequate or failed internal processes, people, and systems, or from external events.

transactions with credit weaknesses to help prevent defaults and increase recoveries on transactions that default.

Recovery of Claims: Ex-Im pays a claim when a loan that it has guaranteed or an insurance policy that it has issued defaults. Ex-Im tries to minimize losses on claims paid by pursuing recovery of the amount of claims it paid. For example, it can collect on the assets of the obligors or the collateral for a transaction.

Ex-Im uses a loss estimation model to estimate credit subsidy costs and loss reserves and allowances for these risks. Ex-Im annually updates its loss model, and the model is subsequently reviewed by OMB. The expected loss model calculates loss rates based on historical data (the default and loss history of prior loan guarantee and insurance transactions as well as variables that can be used to predict defaults and losses, such as transaction amount and length, obligor type, product type, and risk rating) and qualitative factors (minimum loss rate, global economic risk, and region, industry, and aircraft portfolio obligor concentration risk) to account for risks associated with the agency's current portfolio. The model calculates a loss rate (the percentage loss that Ex-Im can expect for each dollar of export financing) for each Ex-Im risk rating and product type. The loss rates produced by the model are then used to estimate future cash flows (repayments, fees, recoveries, and claims) for the business Ex-Im expects in the upcoming year. As of December 31, 2012, Ex-Im reported a default rate for its active portfolio of 0.34 percent.[16]

Ex-Im uses OMB's credit subsidy calculator to determine the credit subsidy costs for existing transactions in its portfolio and projected future transactions based on its estimated future cash flows.[17] These credit subsidy estimates are reported in the President's budget. Ex-Im also uses

---

[16]Ex-Im calculates the default rate as the sum of net claims paid on guarantees and insurance transactions and unpaid past due installments on loans divided by disbursements. Ex-Im defines its active portfolio as those transactions for which the maturity date has not been reached or that have reached maturity but are still within the time frame during which a claim can be submitted.

[17]The credit subsidy calculator is the tool issued by OMB for agencies' use to discount future cash flows and calculate credit subsidy costs. In accordance with the Federal Credit Reform Act of 1990, the discount rates in the OMB credit subsidy calculator are based on interest rates for U.S. Treasury securities.

the estimated future cash flows to calculate the loss reserves or allowances—financial reporting accounts for estimated losses—it needs for each new authorized transaction. Each year, Ex-Im adjusts this loss reserve or allowance amount for each transaction using updated estimates of future cash flows.

In addition to these existing procedures, in January 2013, Ex-Im completed a comprehensive revision of its policies and procedures manual that covers each stage of risk management. According to Ex-Im officials, Ex-Im also has been reviewing and responding to several recommendations on risk management from internal and external auditors, OMB, Ex-Im's Inspector General, and GAO. Inspector General and GAO recommendations include performing and reporting of stress testing, retaining point-in-time historical data on credit performance, setting soft portfolio sublimits (informal thresholds for the portion of total exposure within different segments of the portfolio), and establishing a chief risk officer position.[18]

Forecasting Processes Ex-Im Used for Its Business Plan and Other Estimates Have Weaknesses

The Ex-Im Business Plan concluded that the exposure limits Congress placed on the bank in the Reauthorization Act were appropriate, but the exposure forecast model Ex-Im used to justify its conclusion relied on authorization forecasts and assumptions about repayments that have a degree of uncertainty that was not accounted for in Ex-Im's forecast. Based on its estimates of authorizations and repayments, Ex-Im projects its exposure to rise to within $5.1 billion of its $140 billion limit by the end of 2014. Although this exposure is closer to its exposure limit than it has been at year-end in recent years, it supports Ex-Im's conclusion that the congressional limits are appropriate. However, in developing its estimated authorizations for the Business Plan, Ex-Im used the same forecasting process it used for its recent budget estimates, which were between 11 and 42 percent below actual authorizations. Ex-Im used the same assumptions about repayments as it used in previous years, but did not check these key assumptions against previous experience or report the sensitivity of the model to its assumptions. Alternative forecasts using authorizations and repayments estimated based on previous Ex-Im

---

[18]Export-Import Bank of the United States, Office of the Inspector General, *Report on Portfolio Risk and Loss Reserve Allocation Policies*, OIG-INS-12-02 (Washington, D.C.: September 2012); and GAO-13-303. A stress test is a "what-if" scenario that is not a prediction of the expected outcome.

results produce exposure estimates that would be higher than Ex-Im's limit for 2014, raising concerns about Ex-Im's conclusion that its limits are appropriate.

Ex-Im Projects 2014 Exposure to be Approximately $5 Billion below Limit

Ex-Im's Business Plan stated that the exposure limits for 2012, 2013, and 2014 were appropriate and sufficient for the bank to satisfy anticipated demand for Ex-Im financing under current market conditions. Ex-Im forecast that its exposure in 2013 and 2014 would be below its limits by $9.8 and $5.1 billion, respectively, preserving a small buffer for Ex-Im to respond to market changes and unforeseen increases in demand, allow for variance in its estimates, and signal to U.S. exporters and foreign buyers that Ex-Im support would be available for credit-worthy projects. Ex-Im forecast that its year-end exposure would be $105.8 billion in 2012, $120.2 billion in 2013, and $134.9 billion in 2014, below the congressionally determined exposure limits of $120 billion, $130 billion, and $140 billion, respectively (see fig. 3).

Figure 3: Ex-Im Exposure and Exposure Limit, Fiscal Years 2003-2014

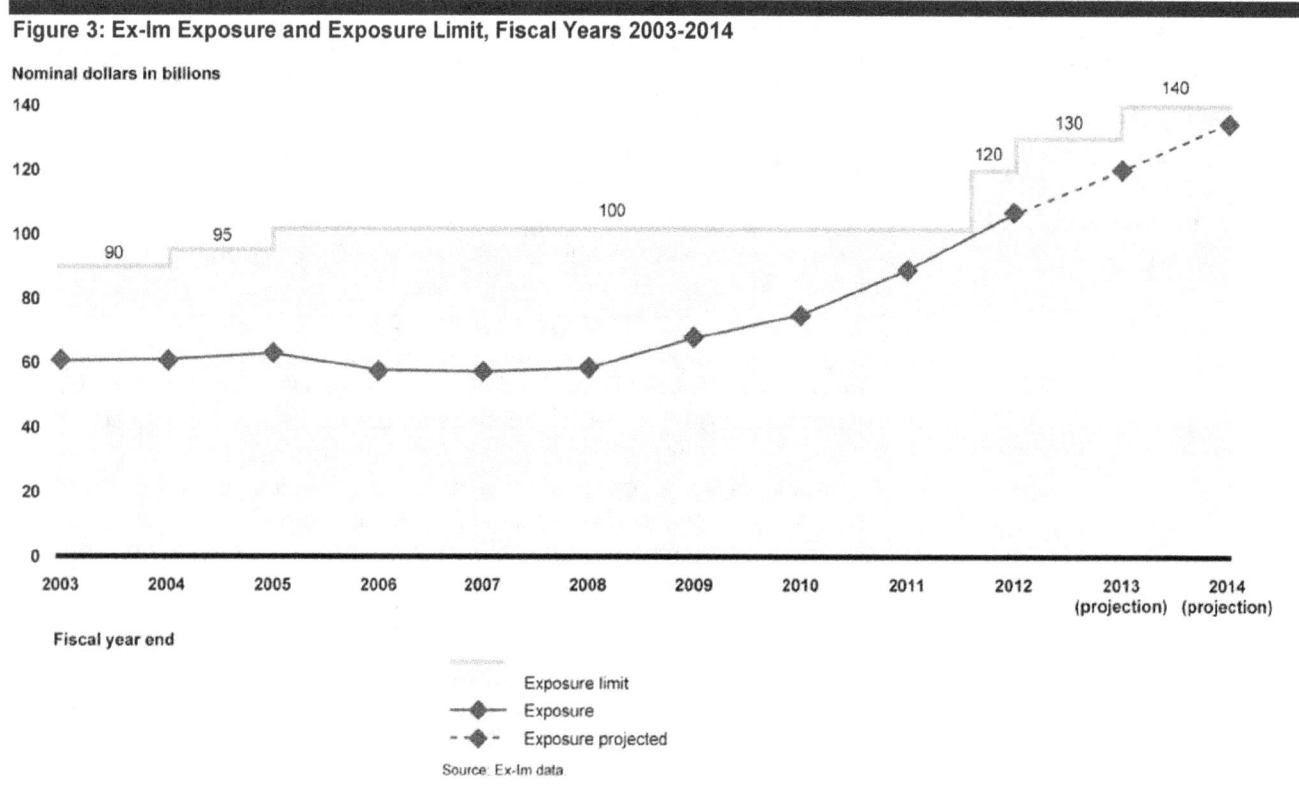

Source: Ex-Im data

GAO-13-620 Export-Import Bank

The buffer between actual exposure and the exposure limit that Ex-Im's Business Plan forecast for 2012, 2013, and 2014 is small in comparison with recent historical experience. Between 2003 and 2008, Ex-Im's exposure hovered around $60 billion, well below its exposure limit. During the fiscal crisis in 2009, Ex-Im's exposure began an upward trend, reducing the buffer between actual exposure and the exposure limit. By the end of 2011, Ex-Im's exposure rose to 89 percent of its limit. At the end of 2012 Ex-Im's exposure limit had increased to $120 billion, but Ex-Im's exposure also increased and remained at 89 percent of the limit. Ex-Im's Business Plan forecasts that further increases will bring exposure to 92 percent of its limit at the end of 2013 and 96 percent at the end of 2014. In dollars, Ex-Im forecasts that it will be $5.1 billion below its $140 billion exposure limit at the end of 2014. According to Ex-Im, at the time of the exposure limit increase from $100 billion to $120 billion (on May 30, 2012), Ex-Im was approaching its maximum permitted exposure and was monitoring its authorizations and repayments but not delaying any authorizations. Although Ex-Im did not have to take such measures at that time, if Ex-Im were to approach its exposure limit in the future, it might need to take actions such as delaying authorizations to prevent exceeding its exposure limit.

A Number of Factors Affect the Accuracy of Ex-Im's Exposure and Authorization Forecasts

The accuracy of Ex-Im's 2013 and 2014 exposure forecasts is uncertain, but the plan's forecast underestimated Ex-Im's 2012 exposure by about $900 million for the 2 months of 2012 remaining at the time it prepared the plan.[19] Ex-Im prepared the plan's 2012 year-end exposure estimate in August 2012. At that time, Ex-Im took its known exposure at the end of July 2012, $99 billion, and estimated the authorizations, repayments, and cancellations that would occur in August and September to determine the year-end 2012 exposure. Ex-Im forecast that $10 billion in additional authorizations in those months would be offset by $3.3 billion in repayments and cancellations—to result in an additional $6.7 billion in exposure in the next 2 months. However, by the end of September, Ex-Im's actual exposure had increased by $7.6 billion, 13 percent higher.[20]

---

[19]As of the end of January 2013, Ex-Im reported actual exposure of $110.8 billion, $9.4 billion below its Business Plan estimate of $120.2 billion for the year end in September and $19.2 billion below its congressionally authorized 2013 limit.

[20]Ex-Im's overall exposure was approximately $106.6 billion at the end of September 2012, $873 million higher than the Business Plan estimate of $105.8 billion Ex-Im made in August 2012.

Ex-Im's authorization forecast for August and September was within 0.3 percent of the actual authorizations in those 2 months, suggesting that the forecast error resulted from an overestimate of the repayments and cancellations that reduce exposure.

Ex-Im's Business Plan forecast $38.4 billion in authorizations in 2013 and $42.7 billion in 2014, with 77 percent of the value of forecast authorizations consisting of long-term transactions including transportation and project and structured finance. According to Ex-Im's Office of the Chief Financial Officer, Ex-Im used the same process to estimate authorizations for the Business Plan that it had used in previous years to estimate authorizations for its annual budget estimates. Ex-Im estimated long-term authorizations in the plan based on an analysis of its pipeline of in-house applications and expected applications, in which customers are in consultation with Ex-Im. For example, Ex-Im reviews aircraft production and delivery schedules to determine when financing for new aircraft is expected to be needed. Long-term transactions have a consultation and application period of between 6 months and 3 years. According to Ex-Im officials, the lead time for the largest project and structured finance transactions is generally at the upper end of this range, giving Ex-Im a more specific basis for its estimates within that time horizon. Ex-Im forecast the average size for individual long-term structured finance transactions in 2013 at $389 million, and $478 million in 2014. Individual transportation authorizations for aircraft included in the 2013 and 2014 forecasts average approximately $266 and $203 million, respectively. The remaining 23 percent of Ex-Im's forecast authorizations are short- and medium-term. Ex-Im estimated these based on information gathered from Ex-Im partner banks—as well as Ex-Im officials' own sense of overall market trends. Ex-Im short- and medium-term transactions averaged approximately $2.2 million in 2012.

Ex-Im's Business Plan asserts that the pipeline approach has been demonstrated to be the most effective forecasting methodology, but also notes that large swings in the amount of transportation and project and structured finance authorizations may occur due to fluctuations in overall market conditions or situations unique to the transaction. According to Ex-Im, it is less likely that authorizations for aircraft or larger project and structured finance authorizations would appear unexpectedly or not occur, but these transactions may be delayed and their amount may fluctuate. Smaller project and structured finance transactions and nonaircraft transportation authorizations may have shorter lead times of several months. Thus, they can be presented to Ex-Im and authorized within 2013 or 2014 without Ex-Im having been aware of them in August

2012, when it prepared the Business Plan. Ex-Im's short- and medium-term transactions generally have shorter lead times than long-term transactions, increasing the uncertainty of Ex-Im's forecast for these transactions in future years. However, because of their generally smaller size, it would take far more change in the number or size of these transactions to affect Ex-Im's overall authorization or exposure estimates.

Since the submittal of the plan in September 2012, the size of some Ex-Im forecast authorizations has fluctuated, as the plan noted could occur. Approximately 6 months after preparing the plan, in February 2013, Ex-Im management reviewed its 2013 authorization forecasts as part of its internal planning. As of March 28, 2013, Ex-Im reduced its 2013 estimate by $2.6 billion (6.9 percent) to $35.8 billion.[21]

Ex-Im reduced its 2013 transportation and structured finance authorizations but did not change other 2013 forecasts.[22] Changes in Ex-Im's forecast resulted from

- transactions no longer expected to be completed in 2013 (decrease of $5.7 billion),
- changes in the size of specific authorizations still forecast to occur (increase of $845 million), and
- new transactions not anticipated at the time of the August 2012 Business Plan forecast (increase of $2.2 billion).

The forecast change in the total amount of authorizations in turn would affect Ex-Im's forecast calculation of exposure. Using Ex-Im's revised authorization estimate, the same model Ex-Im used to support its Business Plan forecast would now predict a reduction of $2.6 billion in exposure in 2013 and $1.6 billion in 2014.

---

[21]As of the end of January 2013, one-third of the way through fiscal year 2013, Ex-Im had authorized $10.9 billion, 28 percent of its Business Plan estimate and 31 percent of its revised estimate. At the same point in 2012, Ex-Im had authorized $7.1 billion—22 percent of its forecast authorizations of $32 billion—but actual authorizations ultimately would total $36 billion.

[22]Ex-Im officials stated that Ex-Im made no change to its 2014 authorization forecast, but plans to assess again the 2014 forecast in approximately June 2013 as part of the development of its 2015 budget.

Ex-Im's Recent Forecasts
Underestimated Authorizations

Ex-Im's data on previous authorizations show that Ex-Im's recent budget forecasts underestimated Ex-Im's authorizations. Ex-Im's 2012 budget estimate, submitted to Congress approximately 16 months before the end of that year, was 11 percent below the actual authorization figure. The 2012 estimate was closer to the actual authorization figures than Ex-Im's forecasts in 2009, 2010, and 2011, which were between 33 and 42 percent below actual authorizations (see fig. 4).

Figure 4: Ex-Im's Estimated Authorizations, Fiscal Years 2008-2014

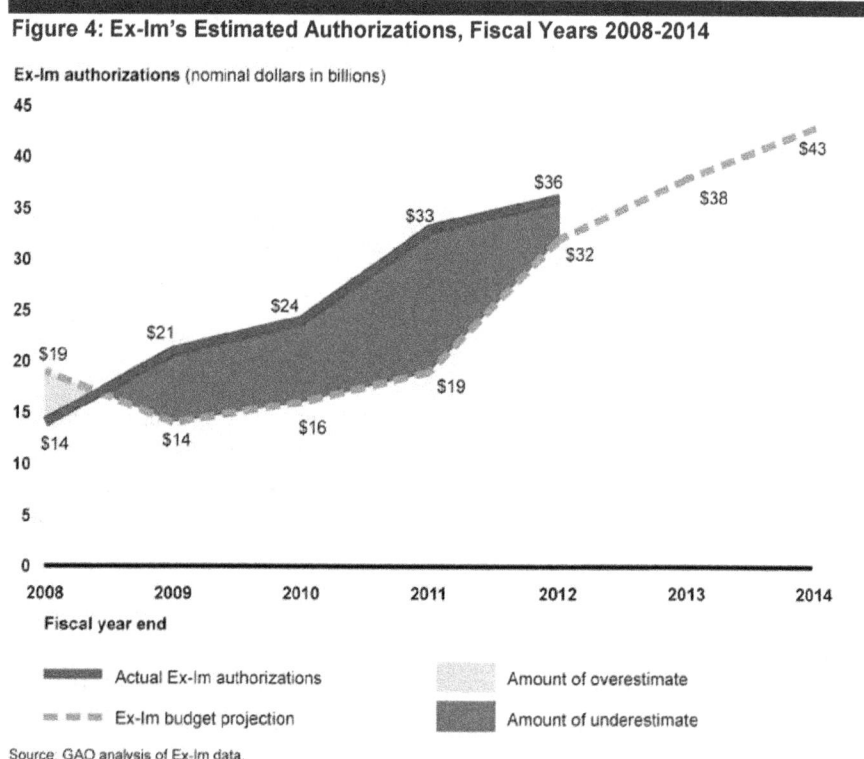

Ex-Im authorizations (nominal dollars in billions)

Fiscal year end

◼◼◼◼ Actual Ex-Im authorizations
▨ Amount of overestimate

= = = Ex-Im budget projection
◼ Amount of underestimate

Source: GAO analysis of Ex-Im data.

Ex-Im's Business Plan notes that few could have predicted the financial crisis of 2007-2009, which led to a significant contraction in commercial lending and a sharp increase in demand for Ex-Im financing. Likewise, the European sovereign debt crisis led in 2011 to a continued need for Ex-Im financing at levels higher than originally estimated. Ex-Im officials asserted that their improved 2012 forecast shows they have begun to better account for the changed economic environment. However, any difference in the amount of authorizations also would affect the forecast amount of Ex-Im's exposure. For example, Ex-Im's 2013 and 2014 forecasts of exposure would increase if forecast authorizations were underestimated by the same 11 percentage points as for 2012. The same forecasting model Ex-Im used to support its Business Plan forecast would now predict Ex-Im's exposure to be $2.2 billion higher at the end of 2013, and $5.9 billion higher at the end of 2014. The estimated total exposure at the end of 2014 would be $140.8 billion, greater than Ex-Im's $140 billion exposure limit for 2014.[23]

Ex-Im Did Not Update or Assess the Assumptions of Its Repayment Forecast Model

Ex-Im prepared the Business Plan exposure forecast in August 2012 using the same model and assumptions about repayments that it had used in previous years. However, the model is sensitive to repayment assumptions and Ex-Im's data no longer support the model's assumption about the percentage of the portfolio that is short-term. To estimate the amount of repayments and cancellations that reduce Ex-Im exposure, Ex-Im made two key assumptions.

- Ex-Im assumed that 30 percent of authorizations each year were for short-term products that would be repaid within the year.
- Ex-Im assumed that the remaining nonshort-term authorizations would be repaid 10 percent at a time over 10 years.

According to the Ex-Im staff who prepared the analysis, the 30 percent and 10-year assumptions were used in previous years and not revised for the Business Plan forecast. However, from 2002 through 2012, the actual percentage of Ex-Im authorizations that were short-term ranged from 24 to 37 percent, averaging 32 percent. These data were available to Ex-Im, but Ex-Im did not use them in its calculations. Furthermore, the percentage of Ex-Im's portfolio that was short-term rapidly decreased in recent years—from 37 percent in 2010 to 31 percent in 2011 and to 25 percent in 2012. The data included in Ex-Im's authorization forecast spreadsheet indicate that Ex-Im would calculate short-term percentages of 22 percent in 2013 and 23 percent in 2014. Using Ex-Im's actual and forecast percentages of short-term authorizations in Ex-Im's model results in a forecast of $123 billion in exposure for 2013 and $142 billion—in excess of the $140 billion exposure limit—for 2014.

---

[23]Even with a shorter time horizon for the forecast, Ex-Im authorization estimates can vary from actual results. In August 2012, Ex-Im estimated that five structured finance transactions greater than $900 million in value would occur in 2013. Approximately 4 months later, as of the end of December 2012, three of these had occurred, and their individual actual values differed from the August projection by between 9 and 11 percent.

While Ex-Im assumes that nonshort-term exposures would be repaid over 10 years, the repayment terms for Ex-Im's long-term products range from 7 to 18 years. Assuming a 9-year average repayment term decreases Ex-Im's exposure by approximately $1 billion at the end of 2014. Assuming an 11-year average repayment term increases the estimate by approximately $1 billion. In combination, varying the model's assumptions about the percentage of short-term authorizations in Ex-Im's portfolio (using a 30 percent assumption or actual historical data) and average repayment terms (9 or 11 years) results in a range of 2014 exposure estimates between $132 billion and $144 billion (see fig. 5).

Figure 5: Range of Ex-Im 2013 and 2014 Exposure Forecasts Using Alternative Short-Term Percentage and Repayment Term Assumptions, Fiscal Years 2011-2014

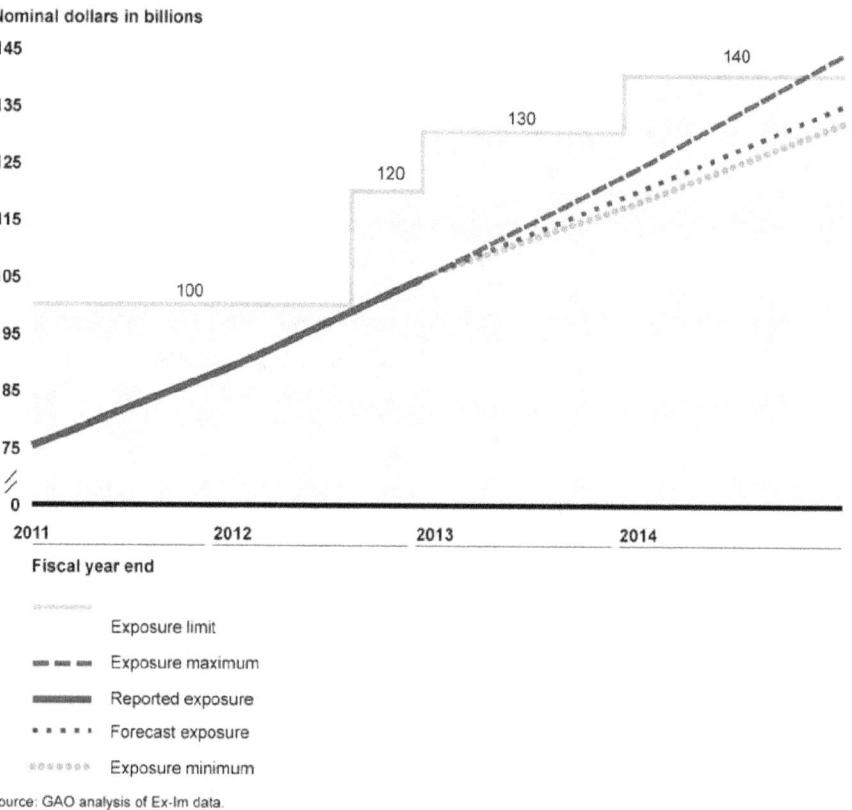

Source: GAO analysis of Ex-Im data.

Although the authorization forecast is uncertain and key assumptions about repayments affect the results, Ex-Im did not conduct sensitivity analyses to assess and report the range of various outcomes. In addition, Ex-Im did not update its model or reassess its process for estimating authorizations in light of previous underestimates. GAO guidance for estimating costs states that assumptions should be realistic, valid, and backed up by historical data to minimize uncertainty and risk.[24] Further, forecast models should be assessed against historical experience to check their validity. In addition, a sensitivity assessment should be conducted for all estimates to examine the effect of changing assumptions, and this assessment should be documented and presented to management. As a result of not addressing the uncertainty of authorization estimates and assumptions in its forecast model, the range of uncertainty of its exposure forecast shows that Ex-Im could have to take actions such as postponing planned authorizations to avoid exceeding its exposure limit.

Business Plan's Limited Risk Evaluation Suggests Opportunities for Additional Analyses

Ex-Im's support for its evaluation of risk of loss was limited in the Business Plan, with some forecast data not provided in the plan pending approval of key analyses by OMB. While Ex-Im concluded there would be no change to its risk of loss for its subportfolios by product type or relating to the small business, sub-Saharan Africa, and renewable energy mandates, it did not provide conclusions on the overall risk of loss or the risk of loss by industry or key market. Ex-Im also did not present data on historical performance in the Business Plan, although it reported performance data such as default rates in other reports. Additionally, Ex-Im does not routinely report the performance of its subportfolios relating to the small business, sub-Saharan Africa, and renewable energy mandates, although these mandates encourage Ex-Im to undertake transactions in these subportfolios and their performance differs from the overall Ex-Im portfolio.

Mandated Reporting Deadline Affected Comprehensiveness of the Business Plan

According to Ex-Im, the deadline for the Business Plan limited its ability to provide more detailed information on its projected risk of loss. The loss rates Ex-Im annually updates are key to its estimation of its risk of loss. OMB did not approve Ex-Im's model that calculates these loss rates until September 24, 2012, 6 days before the plan's mandated completion date of September 30, 2012. Instead of providing detailed information on its projected risk of loss, Ex-Im's Business Plan described the components of its risk-management program (underwriting, monitoring, claims,

---

[24]GAO-09-3SP.

recovery, and loss reserves) and discussed the two elements it used to assess risks (risk ratings and portfolio concentration). Ex-Im's Business Plan stated that the risk rating element includes (1) the distribution of risks among transactions such as how many are low-, medium-, or high-risk; and (2) the individual transactions' risk rating, which is the most relevant factor in predicting losses, according to the plan. Ex-Im's Business Plan included four portfolio concentration measures—(1) the portfolio share of its top 10 countries, (2) the portfolio share of its top 10 obligors, (3) the distribution of its portfolio by geographic region, and (4) the distribution of its portfolio by industry.

Business Plan Risk Analysis Was Limited

Ex-Im's risk analysis in its Business Plan was limited because it did not provide a conclusion on the overall risk of loss, or risk of loss by industry or key market under the new exposure limit. While the plan provided historical data on overall risk rating and portfolio concentration in 2008 and 2012, such data did not reflect the projected changes of composition or the risks of Ex-Im's subportfolios. Specifically,

- Ex-Im did not project the overall risk of loss under the new exposure limit in future years, but instead referred to historical data showing that the overall portfolio risk rating improved between 2008 and 2012. For example, the overall risk rating improved from 4.23 in 2008 to 3.85 in the third quarter of 2012 (on Ex-Im's scale of 1-11, 1 is the least risky).

- Ex-Im did not project changes in industry concentration or provide a conclusion on how such changes would affect its risk of loss. Instead, Ex-Im presented a comparison of the industry distribution of Ex-Im's portfolio in 2008 and 2012 and stated that the concentration in some industries increased from 2008 to 2012 while others decreased. For example, the aircraft industry marginally increased its share of the portfolio. Ex-Im also asserted that its loss estimation model accounted for such changes to determine the appropriate amount of loss reserves.

- Ex-Im did not provide information in the plan on projected changes in exposure composition by key market or a conclusion on how such changes would impact risk of loss. Instead, the plan discussed changes in portfolio concentration by regions, top 10 countries, and top 10 obligors between 2008 and 2012. The plan also compared Ex-Im's portfolio distribution by region in 2008 and 2012, rather than by countries Ex-Im identified as key markets.

- Ex-Im did conclude in the Business Plan that it expected a favorable impact on risk of loss from changes in product mix as it expected its portfolio to shift towards long-term products, which have the lowest loss rates, according to the plan. However, Ex-Im did not provide information on the composition of exposure by product after this shift.

Business Plan Concluded That Compliance with Congressional Mandates Would Have No Effect on Risk Profile

Ex-Im concluded that its risk of loss associated with complying with the small business, sub-Saharan Africa, and renewable energy mandates under the new exposure limits would not increase. Specifically,

- Ex-Im concluded that there would be no increase to its risk of loss associated with complying with the small business mandate under the new exposure limit because a large share of Ex-Im's small business transactions are short-term and highly diversified across industry sectors and geographic areas. In addition, Ex-Im shares the risks of some of these transactions with the originating banks and obtains collateral to secure the transactions.[25]

- Ex-Im concluded that there would be no increase to its risk of loss associated with complying with the sub-Saharan Africa mandate under the new exposure limit. Ex-Im's rationale was that it primarily engages with profitable companies in growing sectors and well-managed African governments.[26]

- Ex-Im concluded that there would be no change to its risk of loss associated with complying with the renewable energy mandate. Ex-Im's rationale was that its renewable energy transactions have default rates comparable to its long-term transactions, which have the lowest default rates, according to the plan.

---

[25]Ex-Im delegates authority to private lenders to underwrite working capital transactions, a type of short-term transaction.

[26]According to Ex-Im officials, some sub-Saharan African countries are rated by the Country Limitation Schedule as too risky for Ex-Im to offer export financing. However, because of the sub-Saharan Africa mandate, Ex-Im has devoted additional resources to assess the risk of a proposed transaction in a sub-Saharan African country that otherwise would be ineligible. Such reviews assess whether countervailing factors specific to the transaction would overcome the country risk and offer Ex-Im a reasonable assurance of repayment.

Ex-Im Did Not Include Loss Data in the Business Plan, but Reports Some Historical Portfolio Performance in Other Documents

While Ex-Im's strategic plan states that the bank uses default rates to measure risk of loss, the Business Plan did not present any historical default rate data on Ex-Im's subportfolios. Again limited by its lack of final projected loss rates at the time of the Business Plan, Ex-Im did not present any projected loss data in the Business Plan—for example, the estimated credit subsidy costs of its portfolio in the future years—to support its conclusions. However, Ex-Im does report some financial data on historical performance in some of its existing reports, which provide some insight into potential losses.[27] These data include default rates by subportfolio of product, key market, and industry; loss reserves and allowances; and overall weighted-average risk ratings. Examples of such reports include Ex-Im's annual reports, audited financial statements, default rate reports, and internal portfolio status reports.

To provide context for the Business Plan's conclusions on risk of loss, we reviewed fiscal year-end financial data from Ex-Im's active portfolio for 2008 and 2012. Using Ex-Im's default rate methodology, we calculated the average default rates for 2008 and 2012 based on subportfolio-level data Ex-Im compiled at our request. Table 1 shows that the default rates of the subportfolios were generally lower than the overall default rate as of September 30, 2012, with the exception of the subportfolios of medium-term products and transactions with only small business participants.

---

[27]The 2012 reauthorization act requires Ex-Im to submit a quarterly default rate report providing default rates by product, key market, and industry. See Pub. L. No. 112-122, § 6. In response to the congressional requirement, Ex-Im submitted its first default report on September 19, 2012.

Table 1: Ex-Im Average Default Rates by Selected Subportfolio as of September 30, 2008, and 2012

Average default rate	September 30, 2008[d]	September 30, 2012[d]
Overall	**1.1%**	**0.3%**
Four major industries[a]	0.8	0.1
Nine key markets	3.1	0.3
Long-term products	0.4	0.1
Medium-term products[b]	17.5	7.6
Short-term products	0.4	0.2
Small business transactions[c]	3.0	0.5
100% Small business transactions[c]	1.4	1.1
Sub-Saharan Africa transactions[c]	1.1	0.2
100% Sub-Saharan Africa transactions[c]	1.2	0.2
Renewable energy transactions	0.0	0.0

Source: GAO analysis of Ex-Im data.

[a]The four major industries are aircraft, manufacturing, oil and gas, and power projects. Ex-Im included these four industries and a fifth category ("all other") in its annual reports from 2008 through 2012. We requested default rate data for industry sectors listed in the Business Plan. Ex-Im provided data only for these four industries because, according to Ex-Im officials, the exposure amounts of other industries are much smaller than those of the top four industries.

[b]As of the end of 2012, the dollar amount of medium-term insurance transactions represented less than 1 percent of the dollar amount of Ex-Im's active authorizations.

[c]We refer to transactions with only small business participants as "100 percent small business transactions" and those with only sub-Saharan Africa participants as "100 percent sub-Saharan Africa transactions." The designation "small business transactions" refers to Ex-Im transactions that may include small and other businesses. Similarly, Ex-Im has a mult buyer product where some of the buyers may be in sub-Saharan Africa and some may not. Ex-Im tracks defaults by transaction, not by participant; therefore, a default in a mixed transaction may not be attributable to its small business or sub-Saharan Africa components. Furthermore, for small business transactions, the counterparty that may default is not the small business. Thus, a default is not attributable to a particular small business, only to the counterparty that purchases the small business's export.

[d]As we previously reported, the default rate data showing a declining trend between 2008 and 2012 may not be conclusive because Ex-Im's portfolio at the end of 2012 contained a large volume of recent transactions that have not reached their peak default periods. Ex-Im also does not retain point-in-time historical data on credit performance to allow it to compare defaults of recent and seasoned transactions at comparable points in time. We recently made a recommendation to address this weakness, and Ex-Im concurred with the recommendation.

While Ex-Im's average default rates overall and by subportfolio generally declined from 2008 to 2012, the declining trend may not be conclusive because Ex-Im's portfolio at the end of 2012 contained a large volume of recent transactions that have not reached their peak default periods, as we recently reported.[28] Recent transactions have had limited time to default and may not default until they are more seasoned. Further, Ex-Im does not retain point-in-time historical data on credit performance to allow it to compare defaults of recent and seasoned transactions at comparable points in time. We recently made a recommendation to address this weakness so that Ex-Im can conduct future analyses comparing the performance of its portfolio between years.[29] Ex-Im concurred with this recommendation.

Ex-Im Has Not Routinely Reported Risk of Loss Related to Three Congressional Mandates

Business Plan Did Not Provide Risk Rating Data to Support Its Risk Conclusions on Congressional Mandates

While Ex-Im included an assessment of the risk of loss associated with implementing the three congressional mandates in its Business Plan as required by the Reauthorization Act, Ex-Im missed the opportunity to present any risk rating data to support its risk evaluations, though this was not required. Again limited by its lack of final projected loss rates—which are calculated using risk ratings of transactions as a key variable—at the time of the Business Plan, Ex-Im did not present any projected risk rating data in the plan.

While the Business Plan did not include any risk rating data related to the three congressional mandates, to further examine Ex-Im's conclusions on risk of loss associated with complying with the three mandates, we analyzed the weighted-average risk ratings for 2008 and 2012 related to these mandates as compiled by Ex-Im (see table 2). Our analysis shows that Ex-Im's overall weighted-average risk rating declined between 2008 and 2012. However, transactions related to these three mandates generally had higher weighted-average risk ratings than the overall weighted-average risk ratings for both years, except for transactions that partially support small businesses.

---

[28]GAO-13-303.

[29]GAO-13-303.

Table 2: Ex-Im Weighted-Average Risk Ratings Overall and by Small Business, Sub-Saharan Africa, and Renewable Energy Subportfolios, Fiscal Years 2008 and 2012

Weighted-average risk rating[a]	Fiscal year 2008	Fiscal year 2012
Overall	4.25	3.66
Small business transactions[b]	4.10	3.40
100% small business transactions[b]	5.20	4.20
Sub-Saharan Africa transactions[b]	6.20	5.10
100% Sub-Saharan Africa transactions[b]	6.20	5.10
Renewable energy transactions	5.30	4.20

Source: GAO analysis of Ex-Im data.

[a]Risk ratings range from 1 (least risky) to 11 (most risky).

[b]We refer to transactions with only small business participants as "100 percent small business transactions" and those with only sub-Saharan Africa participants as "100 percent sub-Saharan Africa transactions." The designation "small business transactions" refers to Ex-Im transactions that may include small and other businesses. Similarly, Ex-Im has a mult buyer product where some of the buyers may be in sub-Saharan Africa and some may not. Ex-Im tracks defaults by transaction, not by participant; therefore, a default in a mixed transaction may not be attributable to its small business or sub-Saharan Africa components. Furthermore, for small business transactions, the counterparty that may default is not the small business. Thus, a default is not attributable to a particular small business, only to the counterparty that purchases the small business's export.

Ex-Im Could Improve Reporting of Risk of Loss Related to Three Congressional Mandates

Ex-Im did not include risk ratings of transactions supporting the small business, sub-Saharan Africa, and renewable energy mandates in the Business Plan, and has not routinely reported the mandates' performance (for example, default rates) at the subportfolio level. Ex-Im's most recent strategic plan indicates that Ex-Im uses default rates as one of the metrics to measure risk performance. In addition, Ex-Im monitors default rates both internally and in quarterly default rate reports to Congress; however, Ex-Im does not include the default rates for transactions supporting these three congressional mandates in its reports. Ex-Im's annual report documents the weighted-average risk rating of its overall portfolio, but does not provide further breakdown of the risk rating at the subportfolio level. Congress requires Ex-Im's default rate reports to include default rates of its overall portfolio and by subportfolios of product type, industry sector, and key market.[30] However, Ex-Im can analyze additional information about its subportfolios related to the three mandates. For example, according to Ex-Im, although it does not

---

[30] 12 U.S.C. § 635g.

separately track the performance of the small business subportfolio, it tracks the performance of the working capital guarantee and short-term multibuyer insurance subportfolios, which are largely small business products and therefore serve as its proxy of the small business subportfolio. Similarly, Ex-Im does not track the performance of renewable energy transactions but has included them in the overall product category. Additionally, Ex-Im's default rate report includes default rates broken out for countries in Africa, which can be used as a proxy for sub-Saharan Africa transactions.

Our analysis indicates that the performance of the subportfolios related to the three congressional mandates can vary from that of the overall portfolio. For instance, the higher risk ratings of the subportfolios suggest these transactions generally are more risky than Ex-Im's overall portfolio. Although it is not required by Congress, Ex-Im is able to report financial performance information on subportfolios supporting the three mandates, such as default rates and risk ratings. Because Ex-Im does not currently report financial performance data related to these mandates, Ex-Im officials explained that the agency specifically developed new analyses to address our data requests for default rates and weighted-average risk ratings at the subportfolio level.

Congress directs that Ex-Im engage in transactions that support business activities fulfilling these three mandates while maintaining reasonable assurance of repayment.[31] In addition, OMB guidance indicates that agencies should use comprehensive reports on the status of the credit financing portfolios to evaluate effectiveness and collect data for program performance measures such as default rates.[32] Furthermore, federal banking regulator guidance suggests that banks should provide financial performance information by portfolio and specific product type to allow management to properly evaluate lending activities.[33] For example, guidance from the Office of the Comptroller of the Currency and interagency guidance from federal banking regulators suggest that banks and other financial institutions should report performance information,

---

[31]12 U.S.C. § 635 and Pub. L. No. 112-74, 125 Stat. 1191.

[32]OMB, Circular No. A-129 Revised.

[33]Board of Governors of the Federal Reserve, *Commercial Bank Examination Manual* (Washington, D.C.: March 1994). While Ex-Im is not bound by this guidance, it faces similar challenges to regulated private financial institutions in managing risks.

such as default rates, loss severity, and delinquencies, and compare their performance with expected performance on an overall and subportfolio level.[34] Financial performance information on Ex-Im's subportfolio can help inform Ex-Im's risk evaluation and risk-management activities. Moreover, reporting financial performance information would be consistent with federal internal control standards, which indicate that communications with external parties, including Congress, should provide information that helps them better understand the risks facing the agency.[35] By not routinely analyzing and reporting performance information on these congressionally mandated transactions, Ex-Im limits its ability to internally evaluate the performance and default rates of transactions it is specifically mandated to maintain, which in turn hinders reporting of such performance to Congress.

Ex-Im's Business Plan's Resource Analysis Was Limited and Growing Congressional Mandated Targets Challenge Bank Resources

In the Business Plan, Ex-Im's response to the reauthorization requirement to assess its resources was limited and further details were not included pending OMB review of Ex-Im's 2014 budget request. From 2008 through 2012, Ex-Im experienced rapid growth in authorizations while its staff and administrative budget level remained relatively flat. The Business Plan reports that Ex-Im's resources are strained and cannot sustain the bank's current level of activity or meet expected demand in coming years. Although the Business Plan does not give specific details about the resources needed to manage Ex-Im's growing authorizations, other bank documents outline estimated resource requirements in more detail. While Ex-Im's support for small business has grown and Ex-Im forecasts continuing increases, Ex-Im's mandated target will require it to increase small business authorizations by $2.4 billion (39 percent) between 2012 and 2014. The Business Plan reports that Ex-Im expects administrative resource constraints may prevent the bank from meeting its congressionally mandated target for small business export financing and lack of demand may prevent meeting the target for renewable energy export financing.

---

[34]Office of the Comptroller of the Currency, Federal Deposit Insurance Corporation, Board of Governors of the Federal Reserve, and Office of Thrift Supervision, *Interagency Guidance on Asset Securitization Activities*; Office of the Comptroller of the Currency, *Asset Securitization: Comptroller's Handbook*. While Ex-Im is not bound by either set of guidance, it faces similar challenges to regulated private financial institutions in managing risks.

[35]GAO/AIMD-00-21.3.1 and GAO-01-1008G.

Business Plan Reports That More Resources are Needed

The Business Plan states that recent growth has strained Ex-Im's resources, particularly its underwriting and monitoring staff. Although the bank has been able to manage the growth through increased operating efficiencies, its current resources cannot sustain the level of activity expected in coming years. According to Ex-Im officials, although additional information was available, Ex-Im's response regarding its resource needs was limited in the Business Plan because Ex-Im's 2014 budget request had not yet been cleared by OMB at the time the plan was due to Congress.

Ex-Im data presented in other documents demonstrate that while authorizations and exposure grew, its administrative budget and staff level remained relatively flat. From 2008 through 2012, Ex-Im's annual authorizations grew nearly 150 percent. Its administrative budget increased 15 percent, from $78 million in 2008 to $90 million in 2012 (see fig. 6). Over the same period, Ex-Im's staff level, as measured by full-time equivalents (FTE), increased less than 11 percent, from 352 in 2008 to 390 in 2012. In 2008, the ratio of authorizations to Ex-Im staff was $40.1 million per employee. In 2012, the ratio was $90.9 million per employee. Ex-Im has requested additional administrative funds in recent years, but has not received the full amount of its requests.

Figure 6: Ex-Im Administrative Budget Requests and Authorizations, Fiscal Years 2008-2014

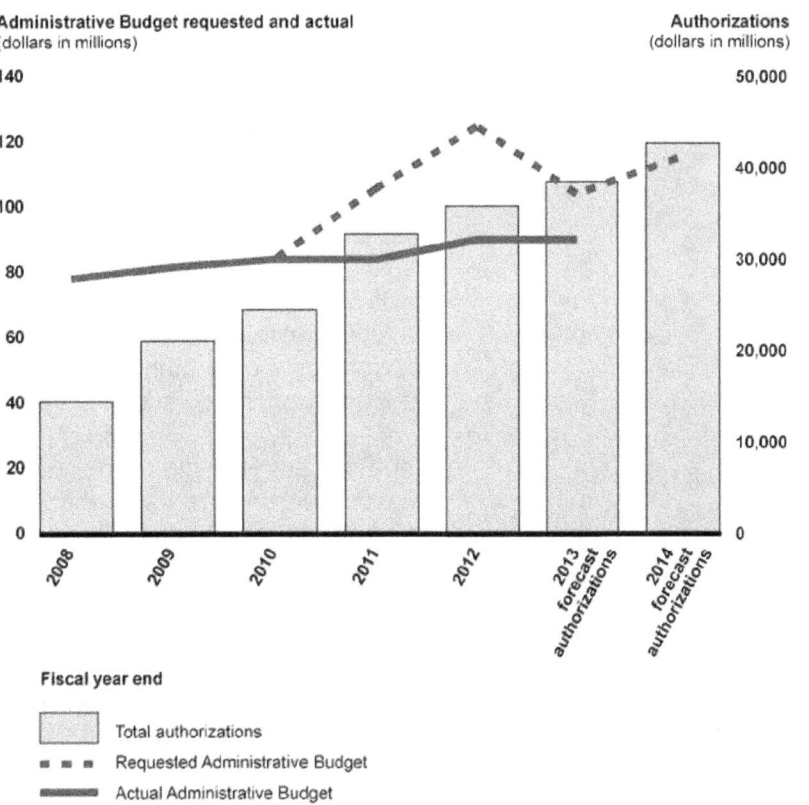

Source: GAO analysis of Ex-Im data and Budget Requests.

According to Ex-Im officials, initially the increased business primarily affected Ex-Im's underwriting function. However, as transactions complete the underwriting phase officials expect workloads to increase significantly in other areas, such as legal and monitoring. In March 2013, we reported that Ex-Im had taken steps to address workload challenges, but had not developed benchmarks for the level of business it can properly support with a given level of resources.[36] We recommended that Ex-Im develop workload benchmarks, monitor workloads against these benchmarks, and develop controls to mitigate risk when workloads

---

[36]GAO-13-303.

approach or exceed these benchmarks. Ex-Im concurred with our recommendation.

Ex-Im does not track the time employees spend on particular tasks. Some Ex-Im divisions are primarily focused on specific transactions—such as small business or transportation—enabling Ex-Im to use the staff and administrative funds allotted to these divisions as a proxy indicator of the resources invested in these transactions. However, other Ex-Im divisions also devote resources to these transactions. For example, Ex-Im staff may spend time underwriting or monitoring various types of transactions in different portfolios. According to Ex-Im officials, systems that track costs more precisely are expensive to develop and require time-intensive data capture. Ex-Im was able to provide the number of direct FTEs that support some of its mandated activities, but did not quantify the FTEs supporting bankwide activities that also support the individual mandates.

Ex-Im Plans to Hire an Additional Analyst to Perform Economic Impact Assessments

The Business Plan did not discuss the bank's ability to conduct economic impact assessments, as specifically mentioned in the reauthorization requirement. According to Ex-Im officials, details of the resources required for economic impact assessments were not included in the plan because Ex-Im was reviewing its economic impact methodology and drafting new guidelines and procedures at the time the plan issued. However, Ex-Im officials stated that they considered the resources needed to conduct these assessments in the Business Plan's assessment of resource needs, particularly for underwriting. Congress requires Ex-Im to consider the economic impact of its work and not to fund activities that will adversely affect U.S. industry.[37] Ex-Im tests for adverse affects by performing an economic impact analysis. As we previously reported, Ex-Im uses a screening process to identify projects with the most potential to have an adverse economic impact, and then

---

[37] 12 U.S.C. § 635(e).

subjects the identified projects to a detailed analysis.[38] According to Ex-Im officials, the bank currently has three staff members conducting economic impact analyses and plans to hire an additional employee to assist with these analyses because Ex-Im expects to conduct more large transactions that will likely require more economic impact assessments.

Projects to Address Information Technology Deficiencies are Underway

The Business Plan describes Ex-Im's information technology (IT) systems as antiquated and inflexible, noting that some systems are more than 30 years old. The plan also states that Ex-Im has begun a Total Enterprise Modernization project to address its IT issues, but notes that continued progress is contingent upon adequate funding. In January 2012, Ex-Im's Inspector General found that Ex-Im's IT infrastructure made it difficult for the bank to provide timely service, effectively manage and track its programs, measure progress, and increase productivity.[39] The Inspector General also found that Ex-Im did not have practices to effectively manage its strategic planning, coordinate initiatives, and determine the best use of funds for improving IT support of its mission.

Ex-Im has been addressing the IT issues identified by the Inspector General. According to initial responses to the Inspector General, dated January 10, 2012, a series of processing system projects were underway. In addition, Ex-Im hired a contractor to evaluate its IT systems and provide recommendations. The contractor's major recommendation was to replace Ex-Im's financial management system. Ex-Im officials expect the new financial system be ready in October 2014.

Ex-Im also has been consolidating different forms into a simplified online form that will guide applicants through the application process and allow

---

[38]GAO, *Export-Import Bank: Improvements Needed in Assessment of Economic Impact*, GAO-07-1071 (Washington, D.C.: Sept. 12, 2007). We reviewed Ex-Im's economic impact assessment process and made recommendations for improving the identification and analysis of applications for economic impact and the transparency of the process. These recommendations included that Ex-Im clarify its procedures for conducting economic impact analyses, create specific methodological guidelines for staff analyzing applications for economic impact, and publish the final determinations on whether a project would have a positive or negative impact. Ex-Im generally concurred with these recommendations and has since issued new procedures and methodological guidelines for assessing economic impact.

[39]Export-Import Bank of the United States, Office of the Inspector General, *Audit of Information Technology Support for Export-Import Bank's Mission*, OIG-AR-12-04 (Washington D.C.: Jan. 24, 2012).

them to sign forms, submit documents, and pay fees online. According to Ex-Im, a pilot form was demonstrated at Ex-Im's annual conference in April 2013 but this project requires OMB approval, which Ex-Im expects by September 2013.

Finally, Ex-Im has been updating its systems to assign each customer a unique identifier recognized across all systems. In its September 2012 update to the Inspector General on the status of IT improvements, Ex-Im projected full implementation by January 2013. However, in March 2013 Ex-Im told us that this upgrade was being tested and was expected to go into operation by September 2013.

Increased Demand for Export Financing Has Driven Mandated Targets Higher

Congress has given Ex-Im explicit policy goals—which include specific targets for small business and environmentally beneficial exports—in addition to its general mandate to support domestic exports.[40]

Despite Large Projected Increases, Ex-Im Projects It Will Not Meet Small Business Mandate

Since the 1980s, Congress has required that Ex-Im make available a certain percentage of its export financing for small business.[41] In 2002, Congress established several new requirements for Ex-Im relating to small business, including increasing the small business financing requirement from 10 to 20 percent of the total dollar value of Ex-Im's annual authorizations. Related congressional directives have included requirements to create a small business division and define standards to measure the bank's success in financing small businesses.

Ex-Im's support for small businesses has increased 92 percent over the past 5 years, from $3.2 billion in 2008 to $6.1 billion in 2012. However, these recent increases have not kept pace with the rising amount—caused by the increase in Ex-Im's overall authorizations—needed to meet

---

[40]For additional information on Ex-Im's congressional mandates, see GAO, *U.S. Export-Import Bank: Actions Needed to Promote Competitiveness and International Cooperation*, GAO-12-294 (Washington, D.C.: Feb. 7, 2012).

[41]Ex-Im interprets the term "make available" as a target that the bank is expected to meet. For more information on Ex-Im support for small business, see GAO, *Export-Import Bank: Performance Standards for Small Business Assistance Are in Place but Ex-Im Is in the Early Stages of Measuring Their Effectiveness*, GAO-08-915 (Washington, D.C.: Jul. 17, 2008).

the 20 percent mandate. Ex-Im projects in its Business Plan that it will be challenged to meet the 20 percent mandate in 2013 or 2014 because the dollar amount of its overall growth will continue outpacing its small business activity. The 20 percent target equaled $4.9 billion in small business authorizations in 2010, the last year in which Ex-Im met the requirement. Based on Ex-Im's projected authorizations, the 20 percent target will equal $8.5 billion in 2014. Therefore, to meet this mandate, Ex-Im will need to increase small business authorizations even further, by $3.6 billion (73 percent) in 4 years. This is also an increase of $2.4 billion (39 percent) from its 2012 small business authorizations (see fig. 7). Small business authorizations accounted for less than 20 percent of the dollar amount of Ex-Im's total authorizations in 2011 and 2012. However, measured in number of transactions, 87 percent of all authorizations approved by Ex-Im since 2008 directly supported small business exports.

Ex-Im expects to increase its small business authorizations by $1.4 billion (22 percent) to approximately $7.7 billion between 2013 and 2014. Ex-Im achieved a similar increase in 2011, but saw a more modest increase of 1.4 percent in 2012 and projects a 2.5 percent increase in 2013. According to the Business Plan's forecast, Ex-Im expects its total authorizations to exceed $42 billion in 2014, which would raise its small business mandate to $8.5 billion. Even if Ex-Im's small business authorizations increase as expected in 2014, the bank still would fall short of its mandated target by more than $800 million.

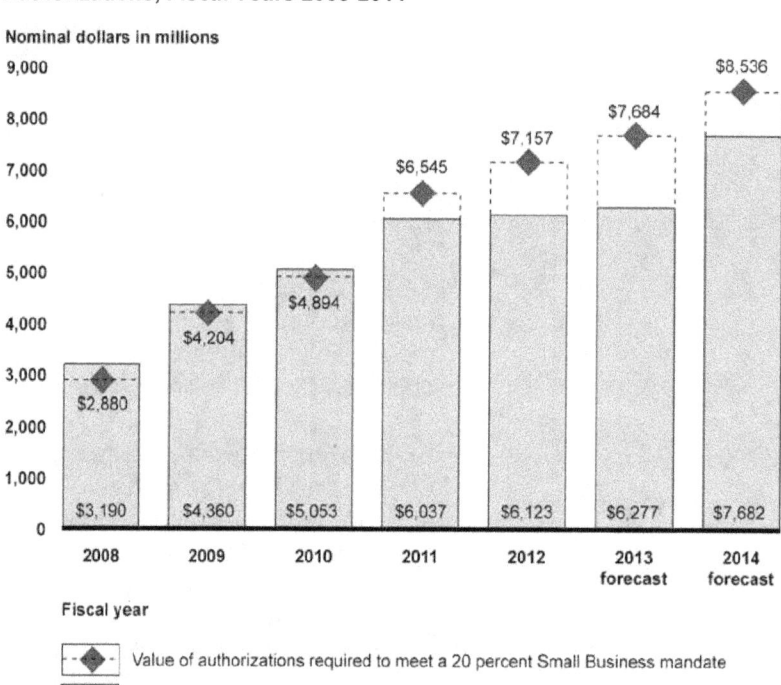

Figure 7: Ex-Im Small Business Mandate Requirement and Actual Small Business Authorizations, Fiscal Years 2008-2014

Nominal dollars in millions

Fiscal year	Actual Small Business authorizations	Value required (20% mandate)
2008	$3,190	$2,880
2009	$4,360	$4,204
2010	$5,053	$4,894
2011	$6,037	$6,545
2012	$6,123	$7,157
2013 forecast	$6,277	$7,684
2014 forecast	$7,682	$8,536

◆ — Value of authorizations required to meet a 20 percent Small Business mandate

▢ Actual Small Business authorizations

Source: GAO analysis of Ex-Im data.

Resources Constrain Ex-Im's Ability to Meet Small Business Mandate

In addition to the rising target amount, Ex-Im officials noted that limited resources will affect its ability to meet the small business mandate. Ex-Im's 2013 Congressional Budget Justification stated that achieving its forecast increase in small business transactions was contingent on an additional $14 million for administrative expenses. Ex-Im planned to use $7 million of the additional administrative funds it requested to support small business outreach and underwriting abilities. However, Ex-Im did not receive this increase.

According to Ex-Im officials, processing small business transactions and bringing in new small business customers is resource intensive. Originating, underwriting, and servicing for small business deals requires more effort than other transactions because small businesses tend to have less exporting experience than larger businesses. Ex-Im's Business Plan notes that small business transactions were approximately $1.8 million on average but required more of Ex-Im's resources than other transactions. For each $1 billion of nonsmall-business authorizations—an amount sometimes achieved with a single Project Finance transaction—Ex-Im must generate $200 million in small business authorizations (about 122 transactions) to meet its small business mandate.

According to Ex-Im officials, 65 of its 390 FTEs are in the Small Business Group and directly support the bank's efforts to meet its small business mandate target. Six additional FTEs from other divisions devote 50 percent of their time to small business transactions. Ex-Im also recently launched several new small business products and opened four new regional offices to support small business exporters.[42] The Business Plan states that Ex-Im has about 25 field staff in 13 offices to support small businesses. Ex-Im also started a series of small business forums and webinars to assist exporters in understanding how the bank's various products could help increase sales. Small business transactions are also supported by dedicated IT resources. For example, Ex-Im has added a small-business portal to its website, which includes step-by-step assistance to exporters, videos, stories about the success of other exporters, and contact information for nearby Ex-Im Export finance managers.

Size of the Renewable Energy Export Market May Constrain Ex-Im's Ability to Meet Mandate Target

Since 1992, Congress has directed Ex-Im to report on its financing of environmentally beneficial exports.[43] In recent years, Congress has provided a 10 percent financing target for environmentally beneficial exports, and in 2009 it directed that the target be specifically for two subcategories of environmentally beneficial exports—renewable energy or energy efficient end-use technologies.

Despite a recent increase in its renewable energy authorizations, Ex-Im's Business Plan indicates that it does not anticipate sufficient market demand to allow the bank to provide enough renewable energy authorizations to meet the target of 10 percent of its overall authorizations and still meet its requirement for reasonable assurance of repayment. Ex-Im's support for renewable energy exports grew from $30 million in 2008

---

[42]In 2012, Ex-Im opened regional Export Finance Centers in Atlanta, Georgia; Minneapolis, Minnesota; and Seattle, Washington. Ex-Im opened an additional center in Detroit, Michigan, in January 2013.

[43]For additional information on Ex-Im support for renewable energy and environmentally beneficial exports, see GAO, *Export-Import Bank: Reaching New Targets for Environmentally Beneficial Exports Presents Major Challenges for Bank*, GAO-10-682 (Washington, D.C.: Jul. 14, 2010).

to $721 million in 2011 and is forecast to reach $1.1 billion in 2014. Although Ex-Im's renewable energy authorizations generally increased since 2008, they have remained less than 3 percent of Ex-Im's overall authorizations. Based on Ex-Im's projected total authorizations for 2013 and 2014, Ex-Im would have to authorize $3.8 billion in renewable energy financing in 2013 and $4.3 billion in 2014 to meet the 10 percent target (see fig. 8).

Figure 8: Ex-Im Renewable Energy Mandate Target and Actual Renewable Energy Authorizations, Fiscal Years 2008-2014

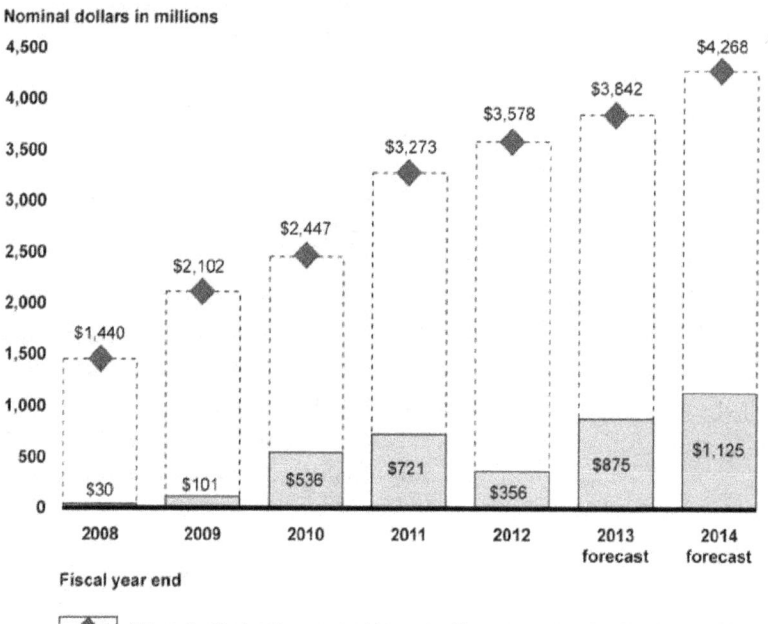

Source: GAO analysis of Ex-Im data.

Ex-Im officials stated that additional administrative resources would not enable it to meet its renewable energy target, as its inability to meet the target results from a lack of demand for renewable energy export financing. Seven bank employees are directly involved in meeting Ex-Im's renewable energy target, six in the Office of Renewable Energy and one in the Structured Finance Group. However, Ex-Im officials noted that a

2010 Department of Commerce report estimated the value of all U.S. renewable energy exports at $2 billion in 2009.[44] Thus, if the bank had financed every U.S. renewable energy export that year, it still could not have met its renewable energy target.

For both small business and renewable energy transactions, the mandated authorization target is tied to total authorizations, which increase or decrease based on factors unrelated to Ex-Im's performance in support of small business or renewable energy. OMB guidance directs agency leaders to set ambitious, yet realistic goals that reflect careful analysis of associated challenges and the agency's capacity and priorities.[45] Communicating this information to external stakeholders, such as Congress, that may have a significant impact on the agency achieving its goals is also consistent with federal internal control standards.

In addition to resources supporting renewable energy transactions, Ex-Im devotes resources to implementing its carbon policy, which was put in place in 2010, and developed in response to a lawsuit challenging Ex-Im's compliance with provisions of the National Environmental Policy Act.[46] The carbon policy (1) promotes renewable energy exports where carbon dioxide emission levels are very low to zero, (2) establishes a $250 million facility to promote renewable energy, and (3) calls for increased transparency in the tracking and reporting of carbon dioxide

---

[44] Department of Commerce/National Export Initiative, Trade Promotion Coordinating Committee, *Renewable Energy and Energy Efficiency Export Initiative* (Washington, D.C.: December 2010).

[45] OMB, Circular No. A–11 Revised, *Preparation, Submission, and Execution of the Budget* (August 2012).

[46] In 2002, Ex-Im's energy financing, specifically its financing for fossil fuel projects, was the subject of a lawsuit brought against the bank and the Overseas Private Investment Corporation by environmental nongovernmental organizations and four U.S. cities. Friends of the Earth, Inc., et al. v. Spinelli, et al. (Civ. No. 02-4106, N.D. Cal.) The lawsuit asserted that Ex-Im and the Overseas Private Investment Corporation provided assistance for fossil fuel projects that caused greenhouse gas emissions without complying with provisions of the National Environmental Policy Act requiring assessments of their projects' impacts on the U.S. environment resulting from their emissions. The lawsuit was settled in 2009 with Ex-Im agreeing to develop and implement a carbon policy for Ex-Im's financing; provide the Board of Directors with additional information about carbon dioxide emissions associated with potential fossil fuel transactions; and take a leadership role in consideration of climate change issues, promoting emissions mitigation measures within the Organisation for Economic Cooperation and Development and among export credit agencies.

emissions. Although Ex-Im's carbon policy was not mandated by Congress, the Business Plan notes that 2012 appropriations language requires Ex-Im to notify Congress of projects that will generate more greenhouse gases than bank-supported projects generated on average during the preceding 3 years.[47] The Business Plan also states that Ex-Im may exceed this threshold as its level of activity increases. Ex-Im has three environmental engineers who directly support compliance with the carbon policy. Additionally, the vice president of Ex-Im's Environmental and Engineering Division and another employee responsible for legal policy spend 20 and 50 percent of their time, respectively, on carbon policy-related activities.

Ex-Im Expects to Meet Its Sub-Saharan Africa Mandate

The sub-Saharan Africa mandate does not have quantifiable targets. This mandate requires Ex-Im, in consultation with the Secretary of Commerce and the Trade Promotion Coordinating Committee, to promote the expansion of its financial commitments in sub-Saharan Africa, establish an advisory committee to assist with the implementation of policies and programs to support this expansion, and report to Congress on efforts to improve relations with relevant regional institutions and coordinate with U.S. agencies pursuant to the African Growth and Opportunity Act.[48] Two employees from Ex-Im's Office of African Development are directly involved in meeting the requirements of the sub-Saharan Africa mandate and half of the duties of an Ex-Im vice chairman are also related to this mandate.

Ex-Im reports that it has met the requirements of this mandate and expects to continue to meet this mandate. Ex-Im's efforts to meet this mandate include: establishing an advisory committee to assist the Board of Directors in meeting Ex-Im's sub-Saharan Africa mandate; and creating a $100 million Africa Initiative to make insurance available for exports to sub-Saharan African countries that otherwise would not be eligible for Ex-Im support. From 2008 to 2012, Ex-Im's authorizations supporting the sub-Saharan Africa mandate increased from $575.5 million to $1.5 billion, and are projected to decline to about $1 billion in 2013 before increasing again to approximately $1.8 billion in 2014.

---

[47]This directive is in the House conference report to the Consolidated Appropriations Act. 2012. H. Rep. No. 112-331, Title VI (112th cong.).

[48]12 U.S.C. § 635(b)(9).

Conclusions

Ex-Im has experienced enormous growth in its authorizations and exposure in recent years, challenging its ability to plan for and manage its portfolio. While Ex-Im may not have been able to anticipate the effect of events like the 2007-2009 financial crisis on its portfolio, the bank also has not reacted to the changed environment and taken steps to account for the uncertainty of its authorization forecasts and reassess its exposure forecast model and assumptions. These assumptions and forecasts should be supported by historical data and experience. In addition, a sensitivity assessment of the effect of these assumptions should be presented to management.

Furthermore, Ex-Im is a demand-driven institution, but Congress has placed specific requirements on the bank's portfolio to support small business, sub-Saharan Africa, and renewable energy. The risk profile of transactions supporting the three mandates differs from the bank's overall risk profile, but Ex-Im has not routinely documented the risk effect of these mandates for its own management or for Congress. Reporting such information would be consistent with OMB and federal banking regulator guidance as well as federal internal control standards.

In addition, the Reauthorization Act and appropriations language reflect important national priorities and congressional interest in supporting small businesses and promoting renewable energy. However, because these requirements are linked directly to the bank's total authorizations, the targets are volatile—subject to fluctuation caused by changes in overall demand for export financing. Recently, the bank's growth has created growing targets that could lead the bank to devote an increasing portion of its limited staff and resources to activities that are particularly time- and resource-intensive, such as small business authorizations, or set goals that may not be achievable in the current market, such as providing a set amount of renewable energy financing that is higher than the demand. OMB criteria indicate that agency targets should be ambitious, yet realistic, and reflect careful analysis, factors affecting outcomes, and agency capacity and priorities. It is important to communicate the effect of these mandated targets on Ex-Im operations to external stakeholders, such as Congress, and the potential impacts percentage-based targets may have on the agency's resources and ability to achieve its goals.

Recommendations for Executive Action

To provide Congress with the appropriate information necessary to make decisions on Ex-Im's exposure limits and targets, we recommend that the Chairman of the Export-Import Bank of the United States take the following four actions:

To improve the accuracy of its forecasts of exposure and authorizations, Ex-Im should

- compare previous forecasts and key assumptions to actual results and adjust its forecast models to incorporate previous experience; and
- assess the sensitivity of the exposure forecast model to key assumptions and authorization estimates and identify and report the range of forecasts based on this analysis.

To help Congress and Ex-Im management understand the performance and risk associated with its subportfolios of transactions supporting the small business, sub-Saharan Africa, and renewable energy mandates, Ex-Im should routinely report financial performance information, including the default rate and risk rating, of these transactions at the subportfolio level.

To better inform Congress of the issues associated with meeting each of the bank's percentage-based mandated targets, Ex-Im should provide Congress with additional information on the resources associated with meeting the mandated targets.

Agency Comments and Our Evaluation

We provided a draft of this report to Ex-Im for comment. Ex-Im concurred with all of our recommendations, and stated that it would incorporate our recommendations into preparation of subsequent reports for Congress. Ex-Im further clarified that it would never exceed the exposure limit set by Congress. Ex-Im stated that it monitors exposure on a monthly basis and if necessary on a daily basis and would put in place the necessary processes and procedures to prevent exceeding the limit. We did not intend to imply that Ex-Im would exceed its limit, but rather that not accounting for forecast uncertainty could lead to Ex-Im having to take such steps to avoid exceeding the limit. We slightly modified the language in the summary of our key findings to clarify this point.

We are sending copies of this report to appropriate congressional committees and the Chairman of the U.S. Export-Import Bank. The report is also available at no charge on the GAO website at http://www.gao.gov.

If you or your staff have any questions about this report, please contact me at (202) 512-4802 or evansl@gao.gov. Contact points for our Offices of Congressional Relations and Public Affairs may be found on the last page of this report. GAO staff who made major contributions to this report are listed in appendix III.

Lawrance L. Evans, Jr.
Director, Financial Markets and Community Investment

Appendix I: Objectives, Scope, and Methodology

Our objectives were to examine the extent to which the Business Plan and analyses of the Export-Import Bank (Ex-Im): (1) justify bank exposure limits; (2) evaluate Ex-Im's risk of loss associated with the increased exposure limit, the changing composition of exposure, and compliance with congressional mandates; and (3) analyze the adequacy of Ex-Im resources to manage authorizations and comply with congressional mandates under the proposed exposure limits. For all objectives, we reviewed and analyzed Ex-Im's response in the Business Plan.

To assess the extent to which Ex-Im's Business Plan and analyses justify exposure limits, we reviewed the spreadsheet model Ex-Im used to forecast exposure, and the source data on authorizations and repayments Ex-Im entered into the model. We met initially with Ex-Im staff who prepared the spreadsheet model to review the Ex-Im spreadsheet to understand its structure and formulas. We then received a copy of the model and reviewed it independently. Following our independent review, we met a second time to discuss more detailed questions about the structure, data, and assumptions contained in the model. To assess the reliability of the exposure model, we compared its August 2012 projections of what exposure would be at the end of September 2012 with the actual results in Ex-Im's annual report. To understand the development of the source data on authorizations used in the model, we met individually with Ex-Im officials from its various business units who prepared the estimates. To assess Ex-Im's methods and data in follow-up to these meetings, we requested and reviewed additional written detail on the methodology used for the authorization estimates and source data for individual estimates of long-term authorizations. We reviewed these source data to determine the forecast timing and average size of the estimates, and checked the forecast authorization size against the actual authorization size for authorizations that occurred through March 2013. To assess the performance of Ex-Im's authorization forecast procedures, we compared previous years' projections with actual results. We additionally reviewed Ex-Im's revised authorization estimates, compared the original and revised estimates, and assessed the effect of the revised estimates on Ex-Im's exposure projection by inputting the revised authorization estimates into Ex-Im's spreadsheet model. To assess Ex-Im's forecast of repayments, we compared the assumption Ex-Im used in the spreadsheet to previous data on the short-term percentage of the Ex-Im portfolio. We then calculated Ex-Im's exposure under alternative scenarios based on these previous actual percentages and alternative

assumptions about repayment terms. Finally, we assessed the
procedures and assumptions Ex-Im used in its Business Plan forecast of
exposure against GAO criteria for developing estimates.[1]

To assess the extent to which Ex-Im's Business Plan and analyses
evaluate the risk of loss associated with Ex-Im's increased exposure limit,
the changing composition of exposure, and compliance with
congressional mandates, we reviewed agency data and documentation—
including Ex-Im's financial performance data, annual reports, and
quarterly default rate reports. We also reviewed relevant GAO and Ex-Im
Inspector General reports and interviewed Ex-Im officials responsible for
risk evaluation. To further examine Ex-Im's risk of loss evaluation in the
Business Plan, we examined weighted-average risk ratings from fiscal
years 2008 to 2012 that Ex-Im compiled at our request for subportfolios
supporting congressional small business, sub-Saharan Africa, and
renewable energy mandates. We compared these subportfolio risk ratings
to Ex-Im's overall portfolio risk ratings for 2008 and 2012. In addition, we
examined default rate data compiled at our request by Ex-Im for these
subportfolios and calculated fiscal year-end default rates for Ex-Im's
subportfolios for 2008 and 2012. We compared these default rate data to
Ex-Im's overall portfolio default rate for 2008 and 2012. To assess the
reliability of these data, we reviewed and checked them against previous
Ex-Im reporting. Additionally, we consulted the data review prepared for
another recent GAO report on Ex-Im.[2] We found the data to be sufficiently
reliable for the purposes of providing context for the financial performance
of overall portfolio and subportfolios in each fiscal year. To evaluate Ex-
Im's risk management, we compared its risk management and analysis
practices against federal banking regulator guidance on financial

---

[1]GAO, *GAO Cost Estimating and Assessment Guide: Best Practices for Developing and
Managing Capital Program Costs*, GAO-09-3SP (Washington, D.C.: March 2009).

[2] GAO, *Export-Import Bank: Recent Growth Underscores Need for Continued
Improvements in Risk Management*, GAO-13-303 (Washington, D.C.: Mar. 28, 2013).

performance reporting, Office of Management and Budget guidance on
federal credit programs, and our standards for internal control.[3]

To assess the extent to which Ex-Im's Business Plan and analyses
analyze the adequacy of Ex-Im resources to manage authorizations and
comply with congressional mandates under the proposed exposure limits,
we reviewed Ex-Im responses to previous GAO and Inspector General
audit reports. We also reviewed relevant Ex-Im documents, including the
Ex-Im Charter, 2010-2015 Strategic Plan, Small Business Reports,
Government Performance and Results Act Performance Reports, Ex-Im's
carbon policy and environmental procedures, Ex-Im's economic impact
procedures and methodological guidelines, Congressional Budget
Justifications, annual reports, 2009-2012 Human Capital Plan, draft 2013-
2015 Human Capital Plan, and Ex-Im's workforce and full-time equivalent
data. To assess the reliability of these data, we reviewed and checked
them against previous Ex-Im reporting. Additionally, we consulted the
data review prepared for another recent GAO report on Ex-Im.[4] We found
these data to be sufficiently reliable for the purposes of describing the
growth of Ex-Im's business, size of its workforce, and amount of
administrative funds requested and received from Congress. We also
reviewed relevant GAO, Congressional Research Service, and Ex-Im
Inspector General reports and met with officials from Ex-Im and Ex-Im's
Office of Inspector General. We compared Ex-Im's planning documents

---

[3] See Board of Governors of the Federal Reserve, *Commercial Bank Examination Manual*
(Washington, D.C.: March 1994). See Office of the Comptroller of the Currency, Federal
Deposit Insurance Corporation, Board of Governors of the Federal Reserve, and Office of
Thrift Supervision, *Interagency Guidance on Asset Securitization Activities* (Washington,
D.C.: December 1999). See Office of the Comptroller of the Currency, *Asset
Securitization: Comptroller's Handbook* (Washington, D.C.: November 1997). While Ex-Im
is not bound by any of the guidance cited above, it faces challenges similar to regulated
private financial institutions in managing risks. See also Office of Management and
Budget, Circular No. A-129 Revised, *Policies for Federal Credit Programs and Non-Tax
Receivables* (2000). See GAO, *Standards for Internal Control in the Federal Government*,
GAO/AIMD-00-21.3.1 (Washington, D.C.: November 1999) and *Internal Control
Management and Evaluation Tool*, GAO-01-1008G (Washington, D.C.: August 2001).

[4] GAO-13-303.

against criteria established by GAO, the Office of Personnel
Management, and the Office of Management and Budget.[5]

We conducted this performance audit from November 2012 to May 2013
in accordance with generally accepted government auditing standards.
Those standards require that we plan and perform the audit to obtain
sufficient, appropriate evidence to provide a reasonable basis for our
findings and conclusions based on our audit objectives. We believe that
the evidence obtained provides a reasonable basis for our findings and
conclusions based on our audit objectives.

[5]GAO/AIMD-00-21.3.1; GAO-01-1008G; Office of Management and Budget Circular No.
A-129; and Office of Personnel Management, *Workforce Planning Model* (Washington,
D.C.: 2005), accessed at http://www.opm.gov/policy-data-oversight/human-capital-
management/reference-materials/strategic-alignment/workforceplanning.pdf

Appendix II: Comments from the U.S. Export-Import Bank

EXPORT-IMPORT BANK
OF THE UNITED STATES

May 22nd, 2013

Mr. Lawrance L. Evans
Director, Financial Markets and Community Investment
U.S. Government Accountability Office
Washington, D.C. 20584

Dear Mr. Evans

Thank you for providing the Export-Import Bank of the United States (Ex-Im Bank) with the opportunity to comment on GAO's May 2013 draft final report (GAO-13-620).

As you know the Bank is committed to continuous improvement and transparency. We are pleased that GAO recognized that the data and reports provided by Ex-Im Bank to support your analysis were considered reliable. We also appreciate that GAO recognized that the limited analysis on risk of loss and resource needs were the result of timing issues. The Business Plan was due to the U.S. Congress on September 30, 2012 and the Bank was limited in our ability to fully discuss these topic areas until the Administration had a chance to review, analyze, validate, and approve certain aspects of our revised credit loss models and new budget requests.

Ex-Im Bank has a robust system in place to monitor the Bank's exposure. The Bank's demand projections are dynamic in nature. Such market-based projections may, and likely will, change over time, due to changes in market conditions both domestically and internationally. As you correctly pointed out in the report, actual demand has exceeded forecasted demand in the past. The report also noted that if this happens in FY 2013 and/or FY 2014, demand for export financing could exceed the exposure limitation. Please be assured that Ex-Im Bank would never exceed the exposure limit set by the U.S. Congress in our Charter. The Bank monitors exposure on a monthly basis and if necessary on a daily basis. If the current exposure approached the limitation, we would put in place the necessary processes and procedures so that at no point in time would the Bank exceed the exposure limitation. Please also note that the Bank's most recent review and analysis does not show a higher demand than originally forecasted and presented in the Business Plan.

Ex-Im Bank very much appreciates GAO's cooperative approach to the audit of the Business Plan. This has been a positive experience for Ex-Im Bank in reviewing our methodology and in identifying areas in which the Bank can further enhance or improve our forecasts as well as increase transparency.

811 VERMONT AVENUE, N.W. WASHINGTON, D.C. 20571

The following are Ex-Im Bank's responses to GAO's recommendations:

1. To improve the accuracy of its forecasts of exposure and authorizations, Ex-Im should: compare previous forecasts and key assumptions to actual results and adjust its forecast models to incorporate previous experience; and assess the sensitivity of the exposure model to key assumptions and authorization estimates and identify and report the range of forecasts based on this analysis.

   Ex-Im Bank is committed to continuous improvement. The Bank agrees with the GAO recommendation and as we develop future year budget requests, the Bank will incorporate these recommendations to further improve the accuracy of demand forecasts and exposure levels. The Bank will also provide an updated and revised forecast related to FY 2013 and FY 2014 activity, incorporating these improvements, to the Senate Committee on Banking, Housing, and Urban Affairs and the House Committee on Financial Services. This will be provided to the committees on or before September 30, 2013.

2. To help Congress and Ex-Im management understand the performance and risk associated with its subportfolios of transactions supporting the small business, sub-Saharan Africa, and renewable energy mandate, Ex-Im should routinely report financial performance information, including default rate and risk rating, of these transactions at the subportfolio level.

   Ex-Im Bank agrees with the recommendation. Ex-Im Bank will incorporate default and risk rating information at the subportfolio level in the Default Reports submitted quarterly to the U.S. Congress. The Bank expects that the next quarterly Default Report, June 30, 2013, will have this information.

3. To better inform Congress of the issues associated with meeting each of the bank's percentage based mandated targets, Ex-Im should provide Congress with additional information on the resources associated with meeting the mandated targets.

   Ex-Im Bank agrees with the recommendation. Ex-Im Bank is currently developing an Enterprise Risk Committee (ERC) to foster the development of enterprise risk awareness. One of the first areas that the ERC will examine will be operational risk beginning in FY 2013. As part of this review, the Bank will also analyze and review the resources necessary to meet the mandated targets. This information, subject to the Administration's approval, will be incorporated into future Congressional Budget Justifications (CBJ). The Bank expects that the next CBJ submitted to the U.S. Congress in April 2014, will incorporate this analysis and review.

Ex-Im Bank is committed to continuous improvement and transparency. We have excellent reporting systems and accurate data that the GAO recognized as reliable. Ex-Im Bank will implement, beginning in FY 2013, all of the Recommendations for Executive Action identified in this GAO audit. Ex-Im Bank will report the implementation status to the U.S. Congress and the GAO by September 30, 2013.

Sincerely,

(CFO)

John A. McAdams
Chief Operating Officer
Export-Import Bank of the United States

Appendix III: GAO Contact and Staff Acknowledgments

GAO Contact	Lawrance L. Evans, Jr. (202) 512-4802 or EvansL@gao.gov
Staff Acknowledgments	In addition to the contact named above, Juan Gobel, Assistant Director; Joshua Akery; Anna Chung; Martin De Alteriis; Risto Laboski; Grace Lui; Yesook Merrill; Barbara Roesmann; and Michael Simon made key contributions to this report. Jena Sinkfield provided technical assistance.

GAO's Mission	The Government Accountability Office, the audit, evaluation, and investigative arm of Congress, exists to support Congress in meeting its constitutional responsibilities and to help improve the performance and accountability of the federal government for the American people. GAO examines the use of public funds; evaluates federal programs and policies; and provides analyses, recommendations, and other assistance to help Congress make informed oversight, policy, and funding decisions. GAO's commitment to good government is reflected in its core values of accountability, integrity, and reliability.
Obtaining Copies of GAO Reports and Testimony	The fastest and easiest way to obtain copies of GAO documents at no cost is through GAO's website (http://www.gao.gov). Each weekday afternoon, GAO posts on its website newly released reports, testimony, and correspondence. To have GAO e-mail you a list of newly posted products, go to http://www.gao.gov and select "E-mail Updates."
Order by Phone	The price of each GAO publication reflects GAO's actual cost of production and distribution and depends on the number of pages in the publication and whether the publication is printed in color or black and white. Pricing and ordering information is posted on GAO's website, http://www.gao.gov/ordering.htm. Place orders by calling (202) 512-6000, toll free (866) 801-7077, or TDD (202) 512-2537. Orders may be paid for using American Express, Discover Card, MasterCard, Visa, check, or money order. Call for additional information.
Connect with GAO	Connect with GAO on Facebook, Flickr, Twitter, and YouTube. Subscribe to our RSS Feeds or E-mail Updates. Listen to our Podcasts. Visit GAO on the web at www.gao.gov.
To Report Fraud, Waste, and Abuse in Federal Programs	Contact: Website: http://www.gao.gov/fraudnet/fraudnet.htm E-mail: fraudnet@gao.gov Automated answering system: (800) 424-5454 or (202) 512-7470
Congressional Relations	Katherine Siggerud, Managing Director, siggerudk@gao.gov, (202) 512-4400, U.S. Government Accountability Office, 441 G Street NW, Room 7125, Washington, DC 20548
Public Affairs	Chuck Young, Managing Director, youngc1@gao.gov, (202) 512-4800 U.S. Government Accountability Office, 441 G Street NW, Room 7149 Washington, DC 20548